Institute of Leadership
& Management

superseries

Managing the Efficient Use of Materials

FIFTH EDITION

Published for the
Institute of Leadership & Management

ELSEVIER

AMSTERDAM • BOSTON • HEIDELBERG • LONDON • NEW YORK • OXFORD
PARIS • SAN DIEGO • SAN FRANCISCO • SINGAPORE • SYDNEY • TOKYO
Pergamon Flexible Learning is an imprint of Elsevier

Pergamon
Flexible
Learning

Pergamon Flexible Learning is an imprint of Elsevier
Linacre House, Jordan Hill, Oxford OX2 8DP, UK
30 Corporate Drive, Suite 400, Burlington, MA 01803, USA

First edition 1986
Second edition 1991
Third edition 1997
Fourth edition 2003
Fifth edition 2007

Editor: David Pardey

Based on material in previous editions of this work

The views expressed in this work are those of the authors and do
not necessarily reflect those of the Institute of Leadership &
Management or of the publisher

Notice
No responsibility is assumed by the publisher for any injury and/or damage to persons or
property as a matter of products liability, negligence or otherwise, or from any use or operation
of any methods, products, instructions or ideas contained in the material herein

British Library Cataloguing in Publication Data
A catalogue record for this book is available from the British Library

Library of Congress Cataloguing in Publication Data
A catalogue record for this book is available from the Library of Congress

ISBN: 978-0-08-046431-2

For information on all Pergamon Flexible Learning publications
visit our website at http://books.elsevier.com

Institute of Leadership & Management
Registered Office
1 Giltspur Street
London
EC1A 9DD
Telephone: 020 7294 2470
www.i-l-m.com
ILM is part of the City & Guilds Group

Typeset by Charon Tec Ltd (A Macmillan Company), Chennai, India
www.charontec.com
Printed and bound in Great Britain

07 08 09 10 11   10 9 8 7 6 5 4 3 2 1

Working together to grow
libraries in developing countries

www.elsevier.com | www.bookaid.org | www.sabre.org

ELSEVIER   BOOK AID International   Sabre Foundation

Contents

Contents

Series preface

Whether you are a tutor/trainer or studying management development to further your career, Super Series provides an exciting and flexible resource to help you to achieve your goals. The fifth edition is completely new and up-to-date, and has been structured to perfectly match the Institute of Leadership & Management (ILM)'s new unit-based qualifications for first line managers. It also harmonizes with the 2004 national occupational standards in management and leadership, providing an invaluable resource for S/NVQs at Level 3 in Management.

Super Series is equally valuable for anyone tutoring or studying any management programmes at this level, whether leading to a qualification or not. Individual workbooks also support short programmes, which may be recognized by ILM as Endorsed or Development Awards, or provide the ideal way to undertake CPD activities.

For learners, coping with all the pressures of today's world, Super Series offers you the flexibility to study at your own pace to fit around your professional and other commitments. You don't need a PC or to attend classes at a specific time – choose when and where to study to suit yourself! And you will always have the complete workbook as a quick reference just when you need it.

For tutors/trainers, Super Series provides an invaluable guide to what needs to be covered, and in what depth. It also allows learners who miss occasional sessions to 'catch up' by dipping into the series.

Super Series provides unrivalled support for all those involved in first line management and supervision.

Unit specification

Title:	Managing the efficient use of materials	Unit Ref:	M3.28
Level:	3		

National credit value:	2	Guided learning hours	10–12 (midpoint 11)

Learning outcomes *The learner will*	Assessment criteria *The learner can (in an organisation with which they are familiar)*	
1. Understand how material stocks are acquired, controlled and recorded in an organisation	1.1	Describe how to determine stock requirements in the workplace
	1.2	Explain two consequences of not maintaining optimum stocks in the workplace
	1.3	Identify organisational stores/stock control principles and procedures
	1.4	Outline the organisation's procedures for recording, receipt and issue of supplies
	1.5	Briefly describe why quality standards need to be maintained in the organisation
2. Know how to minimise waste in an organisation	2.1	Identify potential waste in the organisation
	2.2	Outline the techniques and/or methods for measuring and monitoring waste in the organisation
	2.3	Compile a simple action plan to minimise waste in the workplace

Workbook introduction

1 ILM Super Series study links

This workbook addresses the issues of *Managing the Efficient Use of Materials*. Should you wish to extend your study to other Super Series workbooks covering related or different subject areas, you will find a comprehensive list at the back of this book.

2 Links to ILM qualifications

This workbook relates to the learning outcomes of Unit M3.28 Managing the efficient use of materials from the ILM Level 3 Award, Certificate and Diploma in First Line Management.

3 Workbook objectives

All managers have resources at their disposal. It is the way these resources are used and organized that shows up the differences between a good manager and an ordinary one.

Poor managers will continually bemoan their lack of resources. 'If only I had more people (or more time, or more information, or better materials and equipment),' they will say, 'I could do a decent job'. The response to such a complaint is invariably along the lines of:

'The point is: what kind of job can you do with the resources you already have?'

This workbook is all about the management and control of resources. To control a resource, you have to monitor how well its actual performance compares with the planned performance. Managing includes determining objectives and making plans.

We will start by reviewing the types of resource and make a list of nine although, as we discuss, there are various ways of categorizing resources. We'll then consider four in more detail: people; land and buildings; equipment; and materials.

Sessions B and C focus mainly on materials, and especially the problems entailed in the acquisition and storage of these resources. Session B deals with the principles of stock control, rotating and managing stock, the receipt and issue of materials, and stock levels.

In Session C, we concentrate on the purchasing function, planning aspects of materials management, some examples of applied technology in this area, and the security of stock.

Session D deals with waste management.

3.1 Objectives

When you have completed this workbook you will be better able to:

- contribute to the management and control of resources in your organization;
- explain the principles, and some ways of solving the problems, of stores and stock control;
- increase your skills in various aspects of materials management;
- identify risks to physical, human and information resources and have gained some practical ideas and experience with which to guard against them;
- carry out a review of actual and potential waste generation points and take action to reduce waste accordingly.

4 Activity planner

The following Activities require some planning, so you may want to look at these now.

■ In Activity 2 you are asked to consider the way you monitor two specific resources and to suggest improvements in this area.
■ Activity 5 asks you to explain how you might give individual team members more responsibility for the control of resources.

Session A
Dealing with resources

1 Introduction

> 'Your role, as part of the management team – and never forget that that is what you are, and certainly in the eyes of your people – is to maximize the resources at your disposal to the full limits of your authority.'
>
> John Adair, *The Effective Supervisor*[1]

Whether it's getting people to realize their full potential, making the most of limited time, getting work done in a restricted space, or avoiding the waste of energy, the organization of resources is largely what the job of management is all about.

In this session, we will discuss the background to our subject. We begin by classifying the resources used by all organizations.

Next, we consider the steps in the process of obtaining and managing resources, and then go on to review four specific kinds of resource: people; equipment; land and buildings; and materials.

2 The organization's resources

A resource is a source of wealth. For organizations, resources are the means by which goods and services are produced.

[1] The industrial Society, 1989.

Activity 1

Name **three** resources that you use in the course of your work.

_____

_____

_____

There are many kinds of resources, including:

- raw materials used in production processes – metals, plastics, fibres, and components of all kinds;
- machines used in making things;
- everyday materials for everyday activities, such as pens and pads;
- furniture;
- rooms, workshops and offices.

What about you – are you and your team a resource of the organization?

There are several ways to classify resources.

From the point of view of an economist, resources are classified into: land, capital, and labour.

- **Land** is the economic term used to describe all natural resources. Under this category would be included natural raw materials such as mined metals, and the ground on which work is done.
- **Capital** encompasses all non-natural resources, such as money, machinery, buildings and vehicles.
- **Labour** is a term for the human resources of an organization.

Another classification of organizational resources is: money, manpower, machines and materials – the four Ms.

However, it's useful to break down resources into rather more categories than either of these two groupings do. We will list nine different types of resource.

- Materials are components, raw materials (the inputs to a manufacturing process), consumables and other items upon which work may be done, or which aid people in doing work.

Every organization uses materials of some kind or other. Hospitals use syringes, bandages and blood. Caterers use foods and spices. Computer bureaux use disks, toner and paper. All materials cost money, and must usually be stored somewhere, ready for use.

■ **Equipment is all the tools, machines, and other apparatus needed for making and measuring things, for protecting people, for handling information, for supplying power, and for many other applications.**

Items of equipment range from safety helmets to desk-top computers to 600 megawatt generators. Two important points concerning equipment are that (a) it can be very expensive to buy and to run, and (b) it needs human expertise, if it is to be used well.

■ **People are all the employees, including managers.**

You may be surprised that we call people a resource. After all, people are the thinking, caring, decision-making, co-ordinating, hard-working animals known as human beings. Is it unfair to label them a resource? Certainly, like other resources, they cost money, and their services can be bought and sold. But we have to be careful not to treat people as if they were goods or simply a means of production; humans only respond well if you regard them as individuals and handle them with respect.

■ **Buildings are, essentially, anything with a roof and walls.**

Buildings – factories, offices, hospitals, barns, houses, schools, warehouses and so on – are usually the places where work is done and goods are stored. They are expensive, and take up a lot of space.

■ **Land is where buildings are located, and where other work goes on.**

Land is often in short supply, and can therefore be expensive to buy.

(Note that to avoid confusion, we have separated land from buildings. However, in law, 'land' includes not only the surface, but the buildings on it, the ground below and the air above. And as already mentioned, the economist's definition of land is 'all natural resources'.)

■ **Information is the knowledge or intelligence which tells us how to carry out work activities, whom to sell to, what to make, and so on.**

The right information is often difficult to come by, especially at the time we need it. There is always plenty of useless information around, and a great deal of routine information that we need machines to help us process. It is often the best informed organizations that are the most successful.

■ Energy is the capacity to do work.

We get energy from the sun, indirectly in the forms of oil, coal, other combustible matter, and nuclear materials, and directly as solar power. For most organizations, electricity (which is derived from one of the fuels just mentioned) is the main source of available energy. Of course, humans also need energy, which they get from food.

■ Finance is the money and credit that are the funds of an organization.

Without finance, few other resources could be obtained. An organization's funds may come from personal investments, bank loans, government loans or grants, and other sources. Limited companies issue shares to raise finance, and, in a public limited company (plc), these shares may be offered to the public.

■ Time is the most elusive of resources.

Time waits for nobody, is sometimes on our hands, and often flies. We may kill time, yet live to regret it, because we don't have enough of it. Not everyone would agree that time is a separate resource. 'If it is the time of humans we are concerned with,' they say, 'then it's part of the human resource.' But time, like other resources, can be managed, and used economically or wastefully.

So we have listed as resources:

■ materials;
■ equipment;
■ people;
■ buildings;
■ land;
■ information;
■ energy;
■ finance;
■ time.

We should distinguish between resources and **assets**. Not all assets are resources, and not all resources are assets. The word assets is an accounting term meaning: 'the property, together with claims against debtors, that an organization may apply to discharge its liabilities'.

In this workbook, we don't have room to cover all these resources in any depth, so we have some choices to make.

We will set aside the last four (information, energy, money, and time) and briefly review the others (people, equipment, land and buildings, and materials) in this session.

Then, in the next two sessions, we will focus mainly on the acquisition, storage, and allocation of materials and other physical resources.

But first, a word about the management of resources generally.

3 Managing resources

The management of resources involves the following:

1 deciding what you want to achieve

2 making plans to achieve it

3 specifying the necessary resources

4 locating and acquiring those resources

5 preparing the resources

6 controlling and organizing the resources to best effect.

The organization first needs to decide what it wants to achieve: what are its aims and objectives? There may be long-term and short-term objectives. A supermarket chain may have an overall objective to become bigger and more successful than all its rivals. Meanwhile, in the shorter term, it may decide to open three new branches, and so must then plan to acquire the land, buildings, equipment and people necessary for this aim.

The detail of these plans will include precise specifications of all these resources. The organization must answer questions such as the following.

'What resources will exactly suit our needs?'

'To what extent can we afford to compromise, and make do with less than the ideal?'

'Where can these resources be obtained?'

'How much money are we able and willing to spend on each resource?'

Once the resources are acquired, they must be prepared for use. The preparation will obviously vary according to the type and condition of the resource. Land may have to be cleared, buildings renovated, people trained and equipment set up.

Then, once ready, the resources will have to be organized and controlled, in order to get the best from them.

3.1 Monitoring resources

You may be involved in all the steps listed above, but much of your job may consist of controlling resources – the last step. A key part of controlling is in **monitoring** their use.

You have to know, to a more or less detailed level, about the **quantity**, **quality** and **cost** of the resources under your control.

Doing this job well necessitates:

■ keeping in close touch with what your team members are doing: how well they are coping, what problems they are encountering, and so on;
■ knowing whether the equipment your team needs is available, and in good working order;
■ being informed about the materials being used: whether they are in good supply, of the right quality, and are being used efficiently;
■ ensuring that the available workspace is used effectively.

Activity 2 · 15 mins

Following on from Activity 1, be more specific about the resources you have responsibility for. Summarize them under the following headings.

People (e.g. how many, and in what capacities?).

_____

_____

_____

_____

_____

Equipment (e.g. what types, and what level of value?).

_____

_____

_____

_____

_____

Materials (e.g. what kind, and what level of value?).

_____

_____

_____

_____

_____

Land and buildings, if any (e.g. what size areas?).

_____

_____

_____

_____

_____

Now think about the steps you take to monitor **two** specific resources under your control.

Specific resource 1: _____

How do you monitor the use of this resource, and at what intervals?

_____

_____

_____

If you identify a problem, what do you do about it, and whom do you notify?

_____

_____

_____

Specific resource 2: _____

How do you monitor the use of this resource, and at what intervals?

_____

_____

_____

If you identify a problem, what do you do about it, and whom do you notify?

Now suggest at least **one** way in which the monitoring of one of these resources could be improved. Be as detailed as you can in your answer.

_____

_____

_____

_____

_____

_____

_____

_____

_____

_____

Now we will look at each of four resources in turn: people; equipment; land and buildings; materials.

4 People as a resource

There is sometimes some reluctance to see people as a resource. Hard-nosed senior managers may see them principally as a cost. Others may think that to regard people as a resource is to see them in the same way as materials or machines. But they **are** a resource and one that is critical to success.

Activity 3

3 mins

How can an organization approach the problem of 'specifying' the people it needs?

_____

_____

_____

_____

_____

Most organizations will first decide on the jobs they want done, and the abilities they think are likely to be needed to do them. Generally, organizations are less likely to define personal attributes such as 'Must have brown hair, blue eyes, and good table manners', which could be discriminatory, in any case.

To that end, a job description or specification is normally drawn up. The organization then tries to attract candidates who are likely to be capable of doing that job competently. In many ways, the process isn't far different from buying a piece of equipment. You don't usually start by naming a particular supplier; instead, you decide what you want the equipment to do, and then see which equipment on offer would provide the best value.

But, even before any thought is given to acquiring new people, the organization must analyse objectives, and break the overall task into 'person-sized' pieces. For example, before a school can work out how many teachers it should employ, and with which skills, it will need to know:

- the number of pupils it is expecting to house;
- which subjects must be taught, and at what level;
- how many periods one teacher can cover in a week;

and so on.

With people, as with any other resource, it's a question of the following.

- What do we want to achieve?
- Which activities will help us get there?
- What resources are needed in order to carry out those activities?
- How can we get hold of those resources?
- How can we get the most from the resources once we have them?

In this brief discussion of people as a resource, we won't go into the subjects of interviewing, recruitment, training, motivation and other aspects of personnel management, which are covered in other Super Series titles.

Instead, let's focus on some of the differences between people and other resources.

4.1 The under-used resource

People are probably the least well-developed resource. As John Harvey-Jones said in *All Together Now*[2]:

> I invariably challenge every company I visit by asking them what proportion of the capability of their people they think they are using. I have yet to meet a single one claiming that they are using as much as a half of their people's capabilities if they were released. We talk continuously about the need to improve our productivity and, God knows, it is a dire need; yet we appear to accept with equanimity that in the world of work we are achieving less than half of our capacity.'

Activity 4 · 3 mins

If this observation is true, what explanation can you give for it? Why do you think organizations find it so hard to release the capabilities of people?

_____

_____

_____

_____

_____

_____

Perhaps you referred back to the comments after the last Activity.

Organizations usually get people to fit the jobs, rather than making the jobs fit the people. That being so, employees can only use certain specific skills, and may have little opportunity to shine in other areas. For example, a child care worker may be a brilliant organizer, but may get paid mainly for his or her social skills, rather than administrative ones. Or a secretary with a flair for tactful negotiation may spend most of his or her time typing letters, because that's the job that needs to be done.

If the team leader or manager is perceptive enough to recognize underdeveloped or unused abilities in individual team members, the next problem is to find

[2] Mandarin Paperbacks, 1995.

ways of using them. That's not often easy. There have been instances of organizations branching off in a new direction, when its management realized it had a pool of hidden talent in its midst, but these occasions are rare. You may have sometimes found yourself in the position of having to realize certain aims, and making the best use of available resources in doing so. The only options are in matching a given set of people to a given list of jobs; nothing else is on the agenda.

There are also other difficulties associated with developing people, including:

- the cost of arranging sufficient training, of the right quality;
- motivating individuals, so that they want to work hard and get better at what they do;
- ensuring that jobs are more challenging than boring, but without being too difficult or stressful;
- getting people at all levels involved with decision making, and especially with making decisions about their own jobs.

This last point has been the subject of a great deal of discussion in recent years. You may have come across the word 'empowerment'. Broadly speaking, this means allowing teams and team members to decide the best way of getting their work done, rather than working under close management. The advantages, when empowerment has been carefully implemented and is properly supported, are increased motivation and efficiency.

Activity 5

15 mins

Describe the ways in which you give your team members opportunities to take individual responsibility for the efficient use of resources.

_____

_____

_____

_____

_____

_____

Now explain how you might increase these opportunities.

_____

_____

_____

_____

_____

_____

_____

If you were to give team members more individual responsibility, what effects
do you expect it would have on efficiency and morale?

_____

_____

_____

_____

_____

4.2 Treating people as individuals

Another major difference between people and other resources is that employees should never be regarded as simply a means to an end. Organizations that
treat their people as if they were items of equipment, to be used and set aside
at management's whim, will never get the best from this precious resource.

As Peter Drucker wrote:

> '. . . we habitually define the rank-and-file worker – as distinguished
> from the manager – as a man [sic] who does as he is directed,
> without responsibility or share in the decisions concerning his
> work or that of others. This indicates that we consider the rank-
> and-file worker in the same light as other material resources, and
> as far as his contribution to the enterprise is concerned as standing
> under the laws of mechanics. This is a serious misunderstanding.'[3]

These remarks are also relevant to Activity 4.

To avoid the mistake of regarding employees as objects, we have to realize
that people don't come in bulk packages. Every person is unique, and has an

---

[3] _The Practice of Management_ (1999), Butterworth-Heinemann.

individual contribution to make. Perhaps you think this is so obvious as not to be worth saying. If so, give truthful answers to the questions in the next Activity.

Activity 6

2 mins

How does your organization treat temporary employees? If, say, you hire a clerk, a labourer, or a technician for a few days or weeks, is there any attempt to: (circle your response)

- get to know that person as an individual? YES/NO

- treat the temporary employee with the same respect as permanent staff? YES/NO

- give him or her as much support as other staff? YES/NO

- regard the person as someone who needs motivation and job satisfaction? YES/NO

Perhaps you were able to answer 'yes' to all these questions. It is not unknown, however, for temporary employees (and permanent ones) to be regarded by management and other staff as if they were subhuman – things rather than people.

It would be easy to fill this workbook with discussions on the subject of people resource management, but that is not our main aim. We must move on to other topics.

5 Equipment as a resource

Equipment is a term encompassing various kinds of clothing, tools and machinery. It is by its nature technical, being based on one or more kinds of technology. The word 'technology' has itself been defined as:

'the practical application of methods for using physical resources'.

Technology and competition

Now, even people with little technical knowledge recognize that technology is liable to become outdated very quickly. This fact poses many problems for work organizations. Because of competition, few organizations can afford to become complacent about their methods of producing goods or services, or the systems used in their internal processes. Every organization has to continually find new answers to the following questions.

- How can we raise our quality?
- How can we lower our costs?
- How can we improve our methods?
- How can we do things better than we are doing now?

The drive for increased efficiency and effectiveness often leads down the path of either new technology, or improved methods for utilizing existing technology.

We'll look at some examples of the way in which technology is used in materials management, later in the workbook.

Of course, highly technical and up-to-date equipment (such as automated assembly lines; supercomputers; body scanners and other sophisticated medical machinery) is invariably extremely expensive to purchase and to run. This may place organizations in the dilemma of not being able to afford the investment until income increases, and not being able to increase income until the new machinery is installed. The pooling of resources is often one solution, and this is sometimes part of the rationale behind company mergers.

Equipment as a daily resource

Deciding what equipment to obtain, and when and how to obtain it, is one problem for managers. What about the day-to-day difficulties?

Activity 7   4 mins

What problems do you encounter regarding the use and control of equipment in your area? EITHER list **three** or **four** different problems, OR describe **one** particular problem in detail.

_____

_____

_____

_____

_____

_____

_____

_____

As we have discussed, equipment is often both expensive and complex. As such, it needs a special kind of management. If you use the wrong equipment, or use it incorrectly, the result can be a disaster; at best it will make you and your team inefficient. Typical problems include:

- people not being trained to make the best use of equipment;
- machines and other equipment breaking down or becoming worn;
- having insufficient equipment;
- using inappropriate equipment;
- abusing equipment, deliberately or otherwise;
- using equipment incorrectly.

To get the optimum value from equipment, it is important for the people using it to have:

- a good understanding of what it is designed to do;
- training in how to use it;
- a proper system of maintenance;
- an appropriate system of security.

6 Land and buildings as a resource

Under English law, land and premises are held either as freehold or as leasehold estate.

When an organization purchases the **freehold** of a piece of land, it becomes the outright owner. With certain exceptions, it then owns everything beneath the surface and all the airspace above. If the value of the property rises, the freeholder benefits; if it falls, the freeholder may have to sell at a loss. Because they cost such a lot, and because owners are vulnerable to fluctuations in the property market, land and buildings require very careful management.

Leasehold property is held under the terms of a lease. This grants the leaseholder a right to occupy the land for a fixed period of time, typically for 99, 200 or 999 years.

Usually, the lease will impose restrictions on the use to which the land can be put. The landlord may also specify that repairs be carried out by the occupier, and that rates and taxes be paid.

Apart from the use of land to build upon, either to use or to sell, it may be a more direct source of wealth, for a mining or agricultural company, for example.

Although you may not be responsible for your organization's land and buildings, it is quite possible that you are in control of a work area that is part of a building or land resource.

Activity 8 · 5 mins

Try to **list** three aspects you need to consider when managing a work area. To give you a start, equipment access is one consideration.

_____

_____

_____

You may have mentioned the following.

Access to equipment

Where equipment is needed to carry out a task, it should be in a position where team members can get to it without hindrance. The workspace layout should be designed so that the most frequently used equipment is in the foreground, while rarely used items are further from the work area. Again, safety needs to be borne in mind: it can sometimes be unsafe to make equipment too accessible.

Movement of people

For safety reasons, people need to be able to move about freely in their workplace. But they shouldn't find it necessary to make excessive or unnecessary movements, perhaps because materials and equipment are not close to hand. In addition, if individual paths cross too frequently, work processes may become slow and inefficient.

Orderliness and appearance

A well-managed workspace will be free of clutter and dirt, in order (a) to make the work atmosphere more agreeable, and more productive; and (b) to reduce hazards from fire and accidents.

The overall appearance of the workplace will almost certainly have an effect on morale, and on the response of visitors. Polish and paint can work wonders in this regard.

Siting of materials

As with equipment, thought needs to be given to the placing of work materials, with the efficiency of the work team in mind.

Grouping of staff

Should team members with similar types of expertise be situated together, or would 'skills mix' be more efficient? Different teams work in different ways, and each team leader has to consider which would be most effective.

7 Materials as a resource

In the remainder of this workbook, we will be discussing the storage, allocation, and acquisition of materials. Materials are sometimes subdivided into raw materials, components and consumables.

Activity 9 · 3 mins

Of the materials you use in your workplace (some of which you may have listed in Activity 2), jot down the name of **one** type of consumable, **one** type of component and **one** type of raw material.

_____

_____

_____

_____

_____

_____

_____

Consumables are items that are used up in a work process, and do not necessarily form part of the final product. Examples are cleaning materials, glue, paper documents, masking tape, pens and pencils.

Components are parts, often having themselves been manufactured from raw materials, which go to make a larger assembly. One component of a door is its handle; some of the components of an electric lawn-mower are the rotating blades, the motor, the cable and the on-off switch; engines, wings and fuselage are all aircraft components.

Raw materials are basic substances that are processed in order to manufacture products. Paper is used to make books; silicon is a raw material in the manufacture of transistors; leather is a necessary material for many kinds of shoes; sheet metal is pressed and formed to make car bodies.

Of course, materials are needed in all organizations, not only manufacturing ones. Market gardeners use fertilizer and seeds; transport companies need vehicle spare parts, fuel and log books; financial advisers are likely to use lots of paper and printer toner; locksmiths have key blanks, oil and metal parts; county councils use large quantities of all kinds of materials.

The main problem usually associated with the management of materials is in getting them into the right place at the right time, while keeping costs to a minimum. This problem is the focus of our attention in the next two sessions.

Self-assessment 1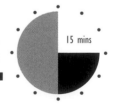

15 mins

1   One classification of resources we discussed was their division into:

- land: the economic term used to describe all natural resources;

- capital: all non-natural resources;

- labour: a term for the human resources of an organization.

How would you match our later list of nine resources against these three? Answer by ticking the appropriate boxes in the table.

	Materials	Equipment	People	Buildings	Land	Information	Energy	Finance	Time
Land									
Capital									
Labour									

2   Fill in the blanks in the following list with suitable words.

The management of resources involves:

1 _____ what you want to achieve;

2 making _____ to achieve it;

3 _____ the necessary resources;

4 locating and _____ those resources;

5 _____ the resources;

6 _____ and organizing the resources to best effect.

3   Complete the following crossword by solving the clues. All the words in the answer were mentioned in the session.

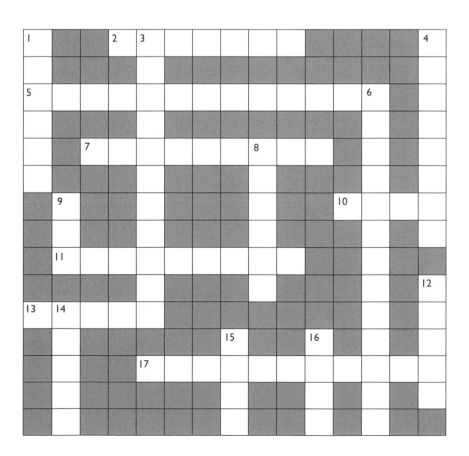

ACROSS

2. Obtain (7 letters).

5. Employment bodies (13 letters).

7. Implements, machines, etc. (9 letters).

10. We don't have enough of it, but we sometimes kill it (4 letters).

11. Where organizations are housed (9 letters).

13. These are useful for making things with (5 letters).

17. There's plenty of this around, but often it's not of the right sort (11 letters).

DOWN

1. A most precious resource (6 letters).

3. Materials that can be used or eaten (11 letters).

4. Resources are the means by which goods and _____ are produced (8 letters).

6. Detailed description of what has to be done (13 letters).

8. The capacity for activity or work (6 letters).

9. Anything one has to do (3 letters).

12. We sometimes make these things before we start work (5 letters).

14. Land and other resources are _____ in short supply (5 letters).

15. Labour, toil, effort or drudgery (4 letters).

16. On which buildings are constructed (4 letters).

Answers to these questions can be found on page 107.

8 Summary

- From the point of view of an economist, resources are classified into: land, capital and labour.

- We listed nine types of resource: materials; equipment; people; buildings; land; information; energy; finance; time.

- The management of resources involves:

  - deciding what we want to achieve;
  - making plans to achieve it;
  - specifying the necessary resources;
  - locating and acquiring those resources;
  - preparing the resources;
  - controlling and organizing the resources to best effect.

- Organizations usually acquire employees after first writing out a job description, defining the skills and other qualities that match the jobs to be done.

- People are frequently an under-developed resource. They are certainly special, and must be treated as individuals.

- To get the optimum value from equipment, it is important for the people using it to have:

  - a good understanding of what it is designed to do;
  - training in how to use it;
  - a proper system of maintenance;
  - an appropriate system of security.

- Although first line managers don't often have to take responsibility for land and buildings, they are often in control of a work area.

- Materials can be divided into raw materials, components and consumables. The main problem usually associated with the management of materials is in getting them into the right place at the right time, while keeping costs to a minimum.

Session B
Storing and allocating materials

1 Introduction

EXTENSION 1
See page 105 for details
of Jessop and Morrison's
useful book.

'The stores should be considered as a temporary location for materials needed for operational purposes, and should be planned, organized and operated in such a way that the period of residence of each item is as short as possible consistent with economic operation. The only reasons for carrying operating stocks is that the material is needed, and that supply cannot be exactly matched with demand.'

David Jessop and Alex Morrison, *Storage and Supply of Materials*

The storing of materials is not a subject that most people give a moment's thought to. A store does not seem to be an interesting place – it's just a location for holding things we want to use later. But for many, perhaps most, organizations, a store is a critical function: badly run, it can bring a company to its knees. The equation is simple: if you try to store too much, you will tie up money in materials unnecessarily, and clog up the stores area; if you try to store too little, the organization's work will be held up waiting for supplies.

We'll start this session with a discussion of the basic principles of stock control. Then we'll go on to the rotation and management of stock, the receipt and issuing of goods, and stock levels.

2 The basic principles of stock control

As we have discussed, all organizations need resources.

So far as materials are concerned, the problem is to get the correct goods, of the required quality, in the right place at the right time.

Obviously, planning is needed in order to achieve this. As these plans proceed, there will come a point when the following can be said.

'We know exactly what we want, and when and where we want it. Now how can we get each specific item in the required place at the specified time?'

Usually, it is the timing that is the most difficult part, and there are typically two ways of answering this question. A very large organization may be able to pass on the problem to its suppliers by using **just-in-time** methods. As we will discuss in Session C, the concept of just-in-time means that the organization is very specific in what it demands of its supplier.

'We want you to supply these goods to a guaranteed level of quality, and to deliver them at precisely the time we can use them – not before or after.'

However, most organizations do not use components and materials at a rate that can justify such a system. Instead they must buy, and take delivery of, materials in advance of when they are needed. They have to check them to see that the goods are of acceptable quality, and then keep them in **stock** by placing them in a storage area, where they can be held in good condition until they are wanted.

It follows that:

stock is a buffer between supply and demand, or between the suppliers and the users.

2.1 The problems of holding stock

The first problem with holding stock is that it is an expense, not a source of profit. A retailer, for example, may have a large warehouse full of first-class merchandise; but it is of absolutely no use until it 'passes the till' and produces some income. Until then, it is a cost: the longer it stays in store, the bigger the cost.

Activity 10

4 mins

What kinds of costs are incurred by keeping goods and materials in store? Try to think of **two** kinds of cost, and say when and how they are incurred.

_____

_____

_____

_____

_____

You may have noted the following points:

- The stock itself is not free: it has to be paid for. The money to pay for it comes from the firm's working capital, and as long as the goods are in store without being sold or used, that capital cannot be used for anything else. This is a nuisance, because that money could be doing something more useful, such as improving handling facilities or training the workforce. If the organization has had to borrow the capital that is tied up in stocks, the interest will have to be paid. If it is the firm's own money, it could have been earning interest.
- Stock needs space, and space costs money. Warehouses and stockrooms have to be designed and built; rent and rates may have to be paid. Racking, handling equipment and control systems have to be bought, installed and maintained. The more space used, the bigger the cost.
- There is also the work involved: the more stock, and the bigger the storage area, the more staff are needed to run and maintain it.
- You may also have thought of another reason why stocks are a cost and an expense: losses and deterioration. Even with the best-organized and best-designed storage facilities, there is a risk of them losing their value – usually called **shrinkage**. The longer the stock remains in store, the greater the risk of losses from these causes. The main causes of shrinkage are:

  - deterioration of quality;
  - date-codes being passed;

- damage;
- pilferage;
- obsolescence.

Activity 11

3 mins

How might a part be made useless through becoming obsolete (that is, going out of date)?

_____

_____

_____

_____

Some, for example the spare parts for old machines, may become useless when the machines are replaced. Others may become obsolete because there has been a change in the law, in industry standards, in a customer's specifications, or in market demands.

To sum up: for all the reasons we have discussed, organizations:

aim to keep the minimum stocks in the minimum space for the minimum time.

What can go wrong when this principle is applied? It is expensive to hold too much stock, but what is potentially even more damaging to an organization is that insufficient goods are available when they are needed. If this happens:

- work may come to a stop;
- people may be laid off;
- sales and customers may be lost.

Having stocks too high is bad news; having stocks too low may be worse news.

Clearly, stock control can be a very important activity for an organization.

Now let's look at stock control with these two main constraints in mind. First, we'll think about ways of reducing the costs of holding stock. One way to do this is to make sure that the oldest stock is used first.

3 Rotating stock

It is very important to make sure that all the goods kept in the stores are in good condition, and that they don't deteriorate or become damaged in any way. It obviously helps to use the oldest stock before the newest. By the 'oldest' we mean the goods that have been in stock the longest.

The technique that demonstrates this principle is referred to as:

first in, first out (FIFO) or stock rotation.

The idea is that the first consignment of a particular item to be received in the stores should also be the first to be issued. The benefits of this approach are that:

- space is made available for newer consignments being delivered;
- the average quality of the items in the store is as high as possible;
- older items do not get lost or hidden by newer items.

There will, of course, be times when it is necessary to use newer stock before old, perhaps because there might be small differences in the newer stocks that affect how they can be used. Nevertheless, FIFO rotation is an important principle for stores management.

A more important reason for rotating stock, however, is to help reduce costs. The oldest goods carry the oldest costs (and prices), and if these are issued before newer goods with higher prices, this will:

- help control the general level of costs
- keep the value of the stocks in line with their 'book' values.

3.1 The two-bin system

The simplest method of stock rotation is the 'two-bin system'. The term 'bin' is used in stores to refer to a particular part of a shelf or a container and, in many cases, a 'bin' may actually **be** a bin. The basis of the system is described in the figure below, and there are many variations to be found.

It is quite common to have a re-order slip or 'bin tag', which is either attached to the reserve bin or prepared when the re-order level is reached. The tag or slip will be passed to the appropriate department to re-order the item.

Stage 1 Main stock placed in bin 1, reserve stock in bin 2 which is sealed. Orders/items picked from bin 1.	1 (main)	2 (reserve)
Stage 2 Bin 1 stock all withdrawn and stock now taken from bin 2, the reserve stock. At the stage of opening bin 2 a new order may be placed.	1	2
Stage 3 Goods delivered. Bin 1 refilled and sealed, so becoming reserve stock.	1	2
Stage 4 Procedure begins once more.		

A variation frequently used with stationery and printed forms is to insert a re-order slip at an appropriate point within the pack. When this level is reached, the re-ordering process will begin.

Activity 12

5 mins

If you can, identify an item of stock from your workplace that is controlled, or could be controlled by a two-bin system. Suggest a reason why this system is suitable for that stock.

_____

_____

_____

_____

The two-bin system is primarily used for items or materials that are:

- standard;
- relatively low unit value;
- regularly or frequently used;
- readily available from suppliers.

The major advantage of two-bin and similar systems is that cost savings are gained. For one thing, records, such as material requisition notes or job cards, are not usually required. Also, stock control labour costs are generally low.

The two-bin system is simple to operate, provided two key questions are answered correctly.

■ What size should the bins be?
■ What triggers the re-ordering process?

If the organization gets these answers wrong, it may have problems with under-stocking or over-stocking.

However, it should be remembered that the vast majority of items stocked at work are not as straightforward as those just described, because:

■ they are non-standard items;
■ usage varies from time to time;
■ supply is not always easy to arrange.

4 Managing stock

A typical system for stock control is shown in the following diagram.

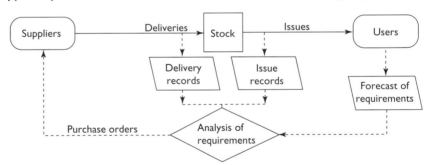

You can see that purchase orders are derived from an analysis of requirements, and that the inputs to this are:

■ a forecast of what the users think they will need;
■ the current stock levels, based on delivery and issue records, and on physical stock checks.

Let's look a little more closely at the way in which stock levels are calculated.

4.1 The book stock formula

By knowing the stock level at a certain time (the 'opening stock'), and recording all purchases and issues, we can calculate the stock at a later time (the 'closing stock').

This formula is the **book stock formula**, and is expressed in the following way:

$$\textbf{opening stock} + \textbf{purchases} - \textbf{issues} = \textbf{closing stock}$$

Here is an example using this formula. If there are 50 reams of paper in stock at the beginning of the month, 100 more are purchased on the 15th of the month and 34 are issued during the month, the closing stock at the end of the month should be as follows.

$$50 + 100 - 34 = 116$$

Assuming the records are accurate, the actual stock level should agree with this figure. This can be physically verified, if required.

Activity 13

3 mins

Complete the following statements.

a At the beginning of the week, 140 disk boxes were in stock. During the week, 120 were delivered by a supplier, and 160 were issued by stores. The closing balance = _____ disk boxes.

b Opening stock + purchases − sales = _____.

c On 1 January, 90 box files were in stock. During the month, 60 were purchased, and at the end of the month 70 were still in stock. _____ files were issued.

d Opening stock + purchases − closing stock = _____.

The answers to this Activity can be found on page 110–11.

4.2 ABC analysis

Because levels of stock are so critical, the stock must be closely managed. Ideally, the organization has to:

■ know how much or how many of each item is in stock;
■ order goods in advance, to take account of the delay between placing an order and receiving the goods (called the **lead time**);

- ensure that there aren't too many of any item, because that costs money;
- ensure that there aren't too few of any item, because that might impede the organization's business;
- be aware of any deterioration, damage, pilferage or obsolescence, as soon as it occurs;
- ensure that stock is used strictly in rotation.

Again, however, we have to make compromises, because management itself costs money. For large stores, it simply isn't feasible to monitor every item this closely. An organization must find the right balance between the cost of controlling stock and the losses incurred as a result of not controlling it.

One way of achieving this balance is to use **ABC analysis**. At its simplest, ABC analysis is a means of categorizing items of stock on the basis of their usage value.

The usage value is calculated in the following way:

usage value = cost of the item × number issued or sold annually

Any store, whether in a hospital, a manufacturing firm, a service company or any other type of organization, will have items ranging in usage value.

For example, a DIY store will stock items ranging from very expensive power tools, to middle-range merchandise such as tins of paint, to small packets of screws. These goods will vary in their popularity, as well as their cost and price.

ABC analysis is a modification of the Pareto principle, or the 80:20 rule as it is often known. Pareto was a nineteenth-century Italian philosopher and economist who showed that the bulk of value is likely to be held by a very small proportion of the total items. While Pareto was originally concerned with wealth, his principle was found to occur in so many other situations that the term 80:20 rule was coined. Generally, for example,

in any store, about 20 per cent of all the items held will account for about 80 per cent of the usage value.

In other words, the Pareto principle suggests the following:

- 20 per cent of the stock produces 80 per cent of the value of sales or issues.
- 80 per cent of the stock produces 20 per cent of the value of sales or issues.

Activity 14 ·

2 mins

Tick which of the following categories should have the greater attention and give reasons for your choice:

a the 20 per cent of the stock that produces 80 per cent of the value of sales or issues. ☐

b the 80 per cent of the stock that produces 20 per cent of the value of sales or issues.

_____

_____

The question was which should have the **greater** attention. Generally, the items in category (a) would be given more consideration because the relatively small number of them produce a far greater proportion of the income. The absence of one item in this category could well have a serious effect on production or customers. However, the items in category (b) may also be important. For example, the effect of running out of invoice forms might be very inconvenient.

The conclusion must be that all items require an effective stock-control system, but that for some the system need not be so complex or costly.

In the DIY store, high-priced power tools may not sell in large quantities, but they are likely to represent a fairly high percentage of total sales. It therefore makes sense to spend more money on accounting for these items, and protecting them from would-be shoplifters, than (say) counting the number of nails in stock. This is not to say that the nails are not worth stocking; instead, it means that the loss of a few nails won't be a great financial loss.

Activity 15 ·

3 mins

To take another example, suppose an office supply company sells 4000 pencils a year costing 55 pence, and sells 150 photocopiers each costing £650. Which has the greater usage value?

_____

The answer is as follows.

cost of pencil	×	annual sales	=	usage value
£0.55	×	4,000	=	£2,200
cost of photocopier	×	annual sales	=	usage value
£650	×	150	=	£97,500

You can see that the photocopier has much greater usage value, even though its annual sales are quite modest.

When the Pareto principle is applied to stock management, we usually adopt three categories, A, B and C, rather than the two categories of 80:20.

- Category A items are those small in number, but high in usage value. They are critical from the financial viewpoint.
- Category B items are medium in both number and usage value.
- Category C items are high in number, but have low usage value.

In a typical workplace, the percentage of items in each of the categories A, B, and C might be as follows.

Category	Approximate % of total items	% of usage value	Comment
A	10	75–85	High usage value, small number – critical: close control.
B	10–30	10–20	Medium number and usage value: medium to close control.
C	50–60	5–10	High number of items, low usage value: less frequent control.

Activity 16

6 mins

In your workplace, try to identify **three** stock items: one of high cost value and low quantity issues or sales; one of medium cost and quantity; one of low cost and high quantity use. Calculate their usage values.

Item 1 (high cost, low quantity)

_____

Item 2 (medium cost and quantity)

_____

Item 3 (low cost, high quantity)

_____

You may have chosen three items close in usage value, but it's more likely that the high cost, low quantity item had the highest usage value, followed by the medium cost, medium quantity item.

ABC analysis consists of the following steps.

1   Calculate the usage value for each item.

2   Rank the items in order of usage value, with the most valuable item at the top.

3   Find the total usage value of all items. Express each item's usage value as a percentage of the total usage value.

4   Calculate the cumulative percentages, working from the top.

5   Classify each item into A, B and C categories by percentage. There is no hard and fast rule for setting boundaries between categories, and this will be a management decision.

The following is a small example, showing how a list of items stocked by a furniture company worked out.

Item	Cost (£)	Annual sales (£)	Usage value (£)	Category
Wall unit	300	1,100	330,000	A
Armchair	125	2,300	287,500	A
Shelving unit	75	2,000	150,000	A
Table	124	1,200	148,800	A
Chair	45	3,000	135,000	A
Bench	155	650	100,750	B
Sofa	173	450	77,850	B
Cabinet	108	560	60,480	B

Item	Cost (£)	Annual sales (£)	Usage value (£)	Category
Chest	230	220	50,600	B
Telephone table	35	400	14,000	C
Carpet rod	2	5,000	10,000	C
Window frame	35	200	7,000	C
Kit of parts	15	450	6,750	C
Wall bracket	22	250	5,500	C
Shelf A	18	300	5,400	C
Shelf B	17	300	5,100	C
Hanger	1	1,200	1,200	C
Bracket	5	200	1,000	C
Holder	4	250	1,000	C
Arm	2	300	600	C

In this case, it was decided to place the items realizing around 75 per cent of the total usage value into category A, another 20 per cent or so in category B, and the rest in category C.

ABC analysis should assist in identifying the amount and nature of attention that individual items require.

Now, we'll move on to discuss two major aspects of storekeeping: receiving and issuing goods, together with the documentation associated with these activities.

5 Receiving goods

What happens when goods are received into stores?

5.1 Essential steps

Whatever industry you work in, the essential steps of receiving goods remain the same.

Activity 17

3 mins

Assume that you work in your organization's stores. Suppose a lorry arrives at the door, and you are told by the driver that he or she has brought some materials for you. What would be the first few things you would do?

_____

_____

_____

_____

_____

_____

EXTENSION 2
Section 7 of the international standard on _Quality Management Systems_, ISO 9001, has a good deal to say about various aspects of stock control, such as verifying materials purchased and maintaining good documentation.

Before they are unloaded, you should check the following:

■ that the goods really are for your organization, and that they have arrived at the right entrance or delivery point;
■ whether the goods have some hazard associated with them – such materials should be clearly marked, and you may need to arrange for special equipment;
■ what is to be done with the materials: they may be urgently required by someone, or they may be routine items to be placed into stores;
■ the best way to unload the vehicle, while bearing in mind the safety of personnel, and the availability of appropriate unloading gear;
■ that an area is available for the goods to be placed.

Following these preliminary checks, the goods receiving function will typically need to:

■ supervise the unloading of the goods, and their transfer to the correct area;
■ check quantities;
■ check that the goods appear to be in satisfactory condition;
■ check to see that the supplier's documentation is correct, and to record the transaction according to the organization's procedures;
■ arrange for the materials to be inspected.

5.2 Documentation

Most organizations these days have computerized stores systems and we will look at developments in this area at the end of the section. However, it would be useful to look first in some detail at two documents that are normally used in a manual system. This should help you to appreciate many aspects of stores documentation.

There are two possible transactions involved in the receipt of goods:

■ taking in new goods, just delivered by a supplier;
■ taking back old goods, which had been issued and which are now being returned for some reason.

For stores records purposes it is essential that these two transactions do not get confused. In both cases a record must be made of the transaction.

■ **New** goods need to be checked against orders by stores personnel and in many organizations they will need to be notified to the people responsible for purchasing and accounting, so that they can be paid for. A **goods received note (GRN)** is usually completed.
■ **Returns** have already been booked into the stores, paid for and booked out again; however, they still have to be recorded. A **goods returned note** (or debit note) is the document used in this case.

The information that appears on these documents must be sufficient for everybody concerned to understand the full details of transaction.

Although each company will have its own particular design for its goods received notes and goods returned notes, there are a number of pieces of information that must always be shown.

The goods received note (GRN)

These obviously vary from one organization to another but all contain basically the same information.

Activity 18 · 3 mins

Jot down **four** pieces of information you think it is important should appear on a goods received note so that each department can get the information it needs.

_____

_____

_____

_____

The words 'Goods Received Note' should appear in a prominent position, accompanied by the following.

■ **A serial number**

This identifies each goods received note (GRN), and distinguishes it from every other GRN.

■ **The date of the receipt**

Making sure the correct date is on every document helps when tracing materials; sometimes, the time of the receipt is also noted.

■ **For each item received:**

■ the quantity should be recorded – if a delivery is made up of more than one item, each part of the delivery must be checked separately and shortages and surpluses must be noted;

■ the description should be given – the description helps to identify the goods; even when a code is used, a description is used to act as a confirmation;

■ a code number or reference number – in many workplaces, codes are used, to avoid confusion caused by vague or incomplete descriptions. In a code such as 'TRP05/KP/FS': 'TRP05' might refer to the product ('typist's office chair type 5'); 'KP' to the supplier ('Kent Plastics'), and 'FS' may indicate that the goods are to be stored in the 'furniture and stationery stores'.

■ **The order number relating to the delivery**

Sometimes an order is delivered in several batches, perhaps over a number of days or even weeks. The order number is used to match each goods received note with the original order.

■ **The name of the supplier**

In case of queries, damaged goods, and so on, the supplier will need to be contacted.

■ **The signature of the person who checks the delivery**

Normally, only authorized people should be allowed to check in goods.

In addition, there may also be spaces for other items such as:

■ the method of delivery (e.g. rail, van, post, courier);
■ the name of the organization delivering the goods;
■ the exact time of the delivery;
■ the condition of goods when received.

Here is an example of a goods received note that you might like to compare with whatever is used in your workplace.

Toys For You Ltd Tiny Works			GOODS RECEIVED NOTE	
Supplier		Date	Serial No.	
		Carrier	Order No.	
Quantity	Description		Reference No.	
For office use			Counted and checked by:	
Ledger No.		Bin No.		

Activity 19

2 mins

Which people or departments in an organization are likely to need a copy of a goods received note?

_____

_____

_____

_____

The way things are done in your own organization will depend on its size and the way it is run. In a typical large organization:

■ one copy is kept by the stores;
■ one copy is sent to the purchasing department, so they know that the supplier has delivered the goods ordered;
■ one copy is sent to the accounts department, so that payment can be arranged.

Sometimes a copy will be given to the department wanting the goods, to let them know they have arrived.

The goods returned note

All internal departments sending goods back to the stores would need to complete a goods returned note which stores can match up to the original documentation.

If the goods are being returned from outside the organization then stores will need to complete a goods returned note that can be matched up to the original sales order and to any other documentation relating to the return. This might include, for instance, a note from the salesman authorizing the return.

Activity 20

Suggest **two** items of information that should appear on a goods returned note, which do not appear on a goods received note.

_____

_____

As well as a serial number, description of the items returned, and how many were received, there would normally be:

- the reason for the return;
- the department or customer returning the goods;
- the job number (or other reference) for which the goods were originally issued;
- the signature of the manager of the department that returned the goods.

On page 41 is an example of a typical goods returned note.

Copies of the goods returned note may be required by:

- the stores, for re-adjusting the record of what is in stock;
- the person or department who returned the goods;
- the costing department, so that any cross-department charges may be made;
- the appropriate department who produced the goods originally.

Copies are often colour-coded, to help ensure that each department gets the correct copy.

Toys For You Ltd Tiny Works			GOODS RETURNED TO STORE No.	
From Department	Date returned		GRN Reference	
	Date of issue			
Job No.	Supplier		Order No.	
Quantity	Description		Reference No.	
Reason for return			Authorizing signature	
For office use			Counted and checked by:	
Ledger No.		Bin No.		

6 Issuing goods

If you are responsible for a stores function, you will appreciate the importance of providing a first-class service in the issue of materials. This is the most visible aspect of stores work, and it is often the activity by which others in the organization will judge you.

Again, it is helpful to look at the documentation procedures.

As with receiving deliveries, two types of transaction may be involved in the issuing of goods:

■ providing a person, customer or department with the goods they request from stores;
■ returning goods to a supplier, because they are faulty, damaged or unsuitable.

Typically, the corresponding documents are:

■ a **customer order**, or internal **materials requisition**;
■ a **credit note** and **returns note**.

6.1 Materials requisition

Once again, these materials vary in detail between organizations but the key information remains the same.

Activity 21 · 3 mins

Jot down **five** items of information that you think should appear on a materials requisition form.

_____

_____

_____

_____

_____

One version of a materials requisition form is shown below.

Toys For You Ltd Tiny Works	MATERIALS REQUISITION		
	Serial No.		
From Department	Date requested		Date required
Required for job:		Supplier (if known)	
Quantity	Description		Code
For office use		Authorizing signature	

Key items are the:

■ serial number – to identify each individual requisition;
■ date;
■ quantity of each item;

- description of each item;
- code or reference number;
- job or batch number for which the goods are required;
- name of the department making the requisition;
- signature of the supervisor or manager of the department making the requisition.

As with goods received documents, three copies are typically required: the person or department making the requisition needs a copy; as does the stores; and the department whose job it is to cost work also needs a copy.

6.2 Goods returned to supplier

For goods returned to the supplier, we have another document, also sometimes called a 'goods returned note'. This can be confusing, as we can't tell from the name whether the goods are being returned to stores, or to the supplier. We'll call it a **returns to supplier note**.

Activity 22

3 mins

Now list **five** items of information that you would include on a returns to supplier note.

_____

_____

_____

_____

_____

A returns to supplier note should match up with the original order, GRN, and materials requisition. It would usually include:

- a serial number unique to that particular document;
- date of the return;
- quantity of each item returned;
- description of the items returned;
- code or reference number for each type of item returned;
- reason for the return;
- date of the original delivery;
- name of supplier;

■ serial number of the goods received note;
■ original order number;
■ signature of the person authorizing the return.

You might also have included the method of return (post, rail, road transport, etc.) and the name of the company carrying the returned goods.

7 Stock levels

As mentioned earlier, it is a basic rule of stock control that we should keep the minimum amount of stocks that are necessary for uninterrupted operation. This saves money, space and work, and reduces shrinkage.

The **minimum stock** is the lowest possible level you should hold to avoid any danger of running out.

It is not the same as the re-order level: it is lower. Sometimes, a **safety stock** level is set slightly below the minimum stock level. The organization will aim to re-order so that the stock issued during the lead time, while awaiting delivery, does not eat into the safety stock.

Activity 23

Here is a diagram of a theoretical stock level record, as it is affected by issues and lead times.

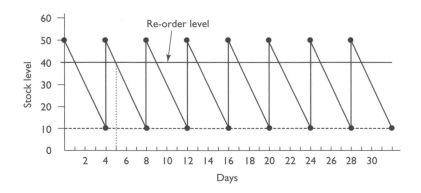

According to this diagram answer the following questions.

- What is the lead time for deliveries? _____

- What is the order quantity? _____

- What is the minimum stock level? _____

This is a very regular pattern – rather unrealistic, in reality – in which the re-order point is a stock level of 40, the lead time for delivery is three days, the order quantity is 40, and the minimum stock level (and in practice, the safety stock) is 10.

In the real world, the rate of use of the stock would vary, so that stock levels would sometimes rise above 40, and the re-order quantity might have to be changed on occasions. Sometimes it would be necessary to use part of the minimum stock. The point of having a safety or minimum stock is that it **can** be used: it is there for use in an emergency. A more realistic diagram is shown below.

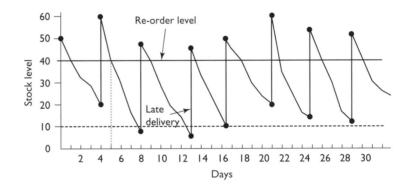

Here, levels are recorded daily, and the delivery period of three days is assumed to start exactly at the time the level reaches 40. You can see that one delivery was late, taking four days instead of three.

▣ 8 Computerized systems

8.1 Computerized receipt of goods

It is usual for goods received notes, goods returned notes and other documents to be generated by a computerized system, and automatically distributed to the various departments, perhaps via email.

In a computerized stores system, the following actions typically take place on receipt of goods into stores.

1 At the point where the goods are received, an operator keys in data giving details of the items.

2 The computer will check to see that this information is valid and appropriate, and, so far as it is possible to tell, that the operator has not made any mistakes.

3 If special actions are necessary, such as inspection or certification, the computer will advise the operator of this fact. It may also pass on this information to others who need to know, by sending messages to their computer terminals.

4 The computer stock records for each item will be adjusted automatically.

5 A goods received note will be generated by the computer, and copies printed out in the areas where they are required. This may not take the form that we have looked at, but may instead be printed or displayed as a summary report of all items received during a certain period.

A very modern system may be even more automated, and involve little, if any, keying in of data or paper printouts. We'll explain this in more detail when we come to the topic of Supply Chain Management in Session C.

8.2 Computerized issue of goods

If the stores system is computerized the person requiring goods will be able to select them from a menu and enter quantities and other specifications as appropriate. This 'electronic requisition' can then be sent to the stores area, just like an internal email.

In the stores area, the message will be automatically processed and relevant information, such as the warehouse location of the item(s) ordered, will also be shown. Orders might be consolidated so that, if three different people have ordered the same item, stores personnel can collect all the orders in one visit rather than wearing their legs out with three visits!

Some systems can devise an optimum 'picking route'. Picking is the name given to the process of extracting ordered goods from their locations in stores: it's a bit like picking the ripe fruit from the trees in an orchard.

Activity 24

5 mins

Below is an illustration showing an extract from a fictional organization's computerized stock requisition system. How could the system be improved?

_____

_____

_____

_____

_____

_____

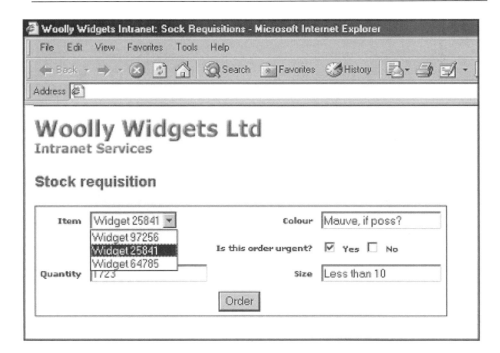

This requisition will probably have to be sent back to the user for clarification, or else the user will receive the wrong part on the wrong date.

- One problem is that users can enter any information they like in the Colour and Size fields. Presumably Widgets are only available in a specific range of colours and specific sizes: the form should therefore offer the user only the options that are actually available.
- The other problem is the Yes/No choice: most people will choose Yes whether or not their need for the item is particularly urgent. It would be much better to force the user to enter a specific date.

You may have identified additional problems, including the title of the screen.

8.3 The use of robots in materials handling

Robots have been employed in industry for a number of years. By 'robot', we mean a machine capable of carrying out a complex series of actions automatically. Robots are especially useful where repetitive but precise movements need to be made.

One example of a robot is the **automated guided vehicle (AGV)**. This is typically employed in moving heavy or palleted goods around a warehouse.

There are a number of guidance systems for AGVs. They may follow the path of:

- wires laid beneath the floor – these wires create a magnetic field that is detected by the steering system of the AGV;
- painted white lines on the floor, the AGV detecting the position of these using light sensors;
- infra-red or visible beams, which are again detected with appropriate sensors.

Alternatively, the AGV may be free-ranging, and kept under control via a computer that sends radio signals.

Activity 25

3 mins

Suggest **two** or more advantages of using robots such as AGVs in materials handling.

_____

_____

_____

_____

_____

_____

_____

_____

Robots such as AGVs hold several advantages where the initial expense can be justified.

■ Robots are able to work for longer periods of time than can people, without becoming tired or bored.

■ Work is generally done more consistently, and faster, than by humans.

■ Their ability to operate with precision usually results in fewer incidents of damage.

■ Robots often improve an organization's health and safety record, as there are fewer humans doing awkward jobs or lifting heavy weights.

8.4 Bar coding

You will no doubt be familiar with the bar code system used to identify and price many types of goods sold in supermarkets and other retail outlets. These consist of a series of dark bars, separated by spaces, as shown in this example.

9 780948 491481

The bars are read by a device that sends a beam of light onto the bar code panel, and detects their reflections, or by a 'light pen' that must be passed across the bar code.

Bar coding is also employed in many industrial applications, for item identification. There are several types of coding in use.

The main benefits that may be gained from using a bar code system include:

■ the speed of recording information;

■ and the level of detail which may be encoded.

8.5 Warehouse management systems

Very modern organizations use a combination of all the technologies above and others, most notably Radio Frequency (RF) systems. An RF system uses portable terminals that have a built in bar code scanner, a small screen and a keyboard. These are either carried by staff or mounted on vehicles or robots.

They are connected via a radio link to the main computer system, including the accounting system and any production systems.

A fully-fledged warehouse management system has many advantages. Although it will be expensive to install it can offer considerable savings.

■ Information about materials movements should be far less prone to error.
■ It is much easier and quicker to locate any item held in the warehouse.
■ Stock levels are updated instantly and perfectly accurately.
■ Orders for new stocks will be placed automatically when needed.

Self-assessment 2

20 mins

1 Explain what is meant by the statement: 'Stock is a buffer between supply and demand.'

_____

_____

_____

_____

_____

2 The following diagram was used to explain the two-bin system, but the words have been removed. Write an explanation in your own words in the boxes on the left.

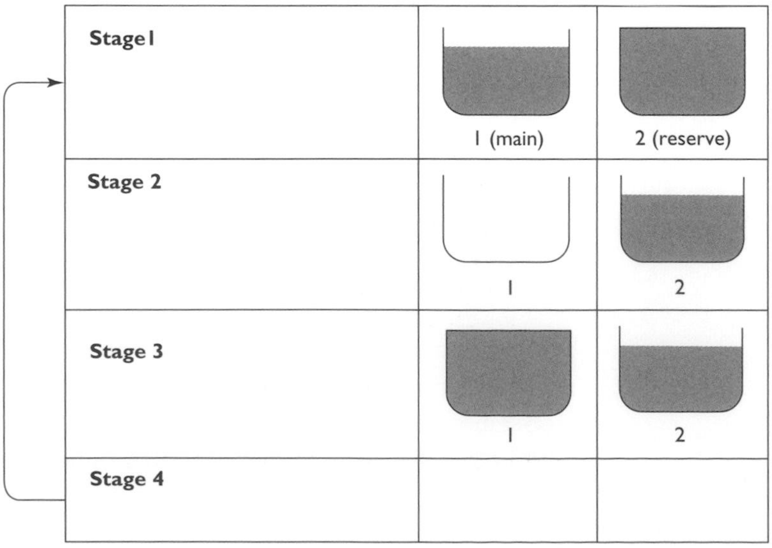

Stage 1		
	1 (main)	2 (reserve)
Stage 2		
	1	2
Stage 3		
	1	2
Stage 4		

3   Work out the usage value of the following items:

Item	Unit cost (£)	Annual sales	Usage value (£)
Vacuum cleaner	230	500	
Microwave oven	340	750	
Refrigerator	175	330	
Installing kit	25	1000	
Spares kit	45	120	

4   Summarize the principles behind ABC analysis, in your own words.

_____

_____

_____

_____

_____

5   Fill in the blanks in the following sentences with suitable words, chosen from the list underneath.

a Stock is a _____ between supply and _____, or between the suppliers and the users.

b Organizations generally aim to keep the _____ stocks in the minimum _____ for the minimum time.

c Having stocks too _____ is bad news; having stocks too _____ may be worse news.

d Opening stock + _____ − issues = closing stock.

e In any store, about _____ of all the items held will account for about _____ of the usage value.

20 PER CENT	80 PER CENT	BUFFER
DEMAND	HIGH	LOW
MINIMUM	PURCHASES	SPACE

6   a What documentation is required when receiving goods? Why do the purchasing and accounts departments need a copy?

b What are the minimum stock level and safety stock level?

Answers to these questions can be found on pages 108–9.

9 Summary

- Stock is a buffer between supply and demand, or between the suppliers and the users.

- There are many costs entailed in holding stocks, and the general aim is to keep the minimum stocks in the minimum space for the minimum time. However, it can be more costly, and more detrimental to the organization's objectives, if stocks are too low.

- To help reduce shrinkage, stock rotation is used. One simple example is the two-bin system.

- The book stock formula is expressed in the following way:

$$\text{opening stock} + \text{purchases} - \text{issues} = \text{closing stock}$$

- ABC analysis is a method of determining the relative amount of attention that should be given to goods in stock. A usage value is calculated for each item, which is the purchase price times the number issued or sold; the highest usage value items then receive the greatest amount of attention.

- Typical items of documentation for receiving goods are the goods received note (GRN), and the goods returned note. For issuing of stocks, the corresponding documents are the customer order or materials requisition, and the returns to supplier note.

- The minimum stock is the lowest possible level you should hold to avoid any danger of running out.

- Where materials management is computerized, the above documents may be issued in the form of a summary report, and automatically routed to the sections that need them.

- The computerized issue of goods can control and consolidate requirements so that stock can be issued with the maximum efficiency.

- The use of technology in materials management also includes robots, bar coding and radio frequency systems.

Session C
Purchasing, resource planning and security

1 Introduction

This last session deals with four aspects of materials resource management.

■ **The purchasing function**

The job of purchasing is to obtain the right materials and other items, of the right specification and quality, from the right source, in the right quantity, at the right time and place, and at the right price.

As such, it is a key function in the organization's management of resources.

We look at some uses of technology that are commonly used to assist the purchasing function: Electronic Date Interchange (EDI), e-procurement and business exchanges.

■ **Materials planning**

We look at two powerful techniques here: just-in-time, and materials requirements planning (MRP).

■ **Resource planning and management**

Computerized methods of resource planning are increasingly practical for many businesses as computing costs reduce because bespoke solutions are no longer always necessary. We consider three software-based tools: Manufacturing Resource Planning, Enterprise Resource Planning and Supply Chain Management.

■ Security

One of the main concerns of resource managers is the security of expensive materials and equipment. Our brief review of this subject is intended to help you apply the principles of good security.

Although these four topics may seem to be unrelated, our discussions of them should help us to tie together some of the themes covered earlier in this workbook.

2 The purchasing function

Let's just remind ourselves of the diagram for stock control, and how the purchasing function fits into the general scheme of things.

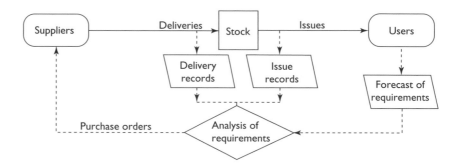

Purchase orders are sent to suppliers as a result of an analysis of requirements. This may happen when:

■ new goods are needed by the users;
■ the re-order level for existing goods is reached.

The existing level may be determined by visually inspecting the stock, but is more often calculated from the records of deliveries and issues.

2.1 The purchasing function

Typical day-to-day purchasing for an individual might involve a quick trip to the local corner shop to buy essentials.

Organizational purchasing (sometimes called '**procurement**') is more like the process you would go through to get the same essentials when you are in a strange town: you'd have to find out where the nearest shop is, find out how to get there, work out the shelf layout, queue for a certain length of time. The process may continue on other days, when you discover that another shop offers lower prices and is quicker to serve you.

Organizational purchasing involves the following activities.

■ Finding suitable suppliers

When a new item is needed, a reliable supplier must be found. Staff who are regularly involved in purchasing will have regular contact with suppliers' representatives, and will usually be able to locate two or three potential vendors fairly quickly.

■ Minimizing the cost of purchases

Invariably, there will be differences in prices between suppliers, for any particular item. It is therefore important that the user or designer provides the purchasing officer with a specification of the goods, including perhaps dimensions, finish, colour, type and so on. Comparisons between suppliers' offerings can then be made on the basis of 'Which product will meet our requirements at minimum overall cost?' Quantity will obviously affect cost, as most suppliers will be willing to give discounts for bulk purchases. The purchasing function has the task of obtaining goods and services on the most favourable terms. Competitive tenders may be invited from contractors for larger value goods.

■ Arranging for goods to be delivered when and where they are needed

Just as important as cost is delivery to 'the right time and the right place'. It is a fact of life that suppliers will sometimes give false information in order to obtain a contract. Experienced purchasing personnel will be wary of promises of delivery dates by unknown or unreliable suppliers.

■ Maintaining good relations with suppliers and with other parts of the organization

Purchasing acts as a link between suppliers and users. Its main task is to provide a service for the rest of the organization, not only in obtaining the required goods, but in giving appropriate advice and information.

Where large quantities are being bought, and the buying organization is spending large sums of money, the supplier–purchaser relationship has to be managed carefully. It is obviously in the interests of both parties to find ways around any problems that may arise, and the purchasing officer plays a crucial role in these negotiations.

Activity 26

3 mins

From the above, what would you say were the benefits to the organization of a well-managed purchasing function? Try to list at least **three** benefits.

_____

_____

_____

_____

_____

_____

If the purchasing function is well handled, the organization should benefit from:

- cost savings, through obtaining goods at lower prices;
- assured supplies;
- lower inventory costs, as a result of having materials at the place and time they're needed;
- good supplier relationships;
- reduced lead times;
- reduced materials obsolescence;
- improved quality control.

2.2 Electronic Data Interchange (EDI)

Electronic Data Interchange (EDI) is the electronic exchange of business documents (purchase orders, invoices, application forms, etc.) from one organization's computer to another organization's computer in standard data formats.

EDI emerged in the **late 1960s** when many industry groups realized that processing the large volume of paper documentation accompanying the shipment of goods resulted in significant delays in settlement and product deliveries.

It is currently estimated that **around 175,000 companies** all over the world (consisting primarily of very large public companies and their numerous trading partners) conduct business using EDI. The list of industries in which EDI is actively used includes shipping, retail, grocery, clothing and textiles, financial, health care and many others. There are three main components of an EDI system (in addition to each organization's own applications, for instance its own accounting system).

■ **EDI standards**

EDI standards eliminate the need for human intervention in the interpretation of incoming and outgoing data. EDI is based on a set of standard formats that define 'transaction sets', which can be used to send basic business data from one computer to another.

These transaction sets replace paper documents such as purchase orders, invoices, and so on. Standards define the structure, format, and content of EDI documents, including the data fields that may be included in a document, and the sequence and format of fields.

■ **EDI gateway**

An EDI gateway reformats outgoing data from an organization-specific format into an EDI standard format and adds data that enables the EDI message to be routed properly to a trading partner.

■ **A communication network**

The main methods of actually communicating the message are through a direct connection, via a Value Added Network Service (VANS) – which is not unlike the Internet except that access is restricted to specific organizations, such as travel agents and airlines – or, in more recent years, via the Internet.

Activity 27

4 mins

We said that EDI standards 'eliminate the need for human intervention in the interpretation of incoming and outgoing data'. What do you think this means and why is it a good thing?

_____

_____

_____

_____

EDI has advantages for the organization ordering goods and for the organization supplying them.

■ The ordering organization enters the details of the order, perhaps using an online catalogue and picking from menu options to save time and avoid errors. The order does not have to be printed out and posted: it is sent via telecommunications and arrives at the supplier's offices almost instantaneously.

■ The supplying organization does not have to transcribe a paper order onto its own computer systems, again, saving a large amount of time and eliminating transcription errors. The incoming EDI order automatically updates the stock system and the accounting ledgers.

2.3 EDI on the Internet

Ever since EDI was first introduced, large companies have always wanted their smaller suppliers to use EDI. But it was far too expensive.

■ Implementing EDI meant purchasing and integrating an unusual combination of software, hardware, and services with an initial cost that could exceed £70,000.
■ Transporting data using private or industry-specific Value Added Network Services (VANS) could cost upward of £15,000 per year.

Trading partners of large companies have faced a tough choice until recently: they could either pay the going price of EDI or lose their large company customer.

Web-based EDI services now present the opportunity for everyone to enjoy the undoubted benefits of EDI services.

■ EDI on the Internet costs less to buy – prices range from free to about £350 per month, depending on usage. For instance, subscribers to IBM's Web-based service pay as little as £25 per month for a subset of EDI services that once cost between 10 to 100 times as much.

■ EDI on the Internet is open and accessible. It is available wherever the Internet is available.

There are, nevertheless, some issues still to be addressed. In particular many companies have substantial investments in their bought-and-paid-for EDI systems and in integrating them with back-end applications. They do not want to retire their systems prematurely, nor do they wish to end up supporting two systems that essentially do the same thing.

2.4 E-procurement or B2B

Many of us have bought a product over the Internet – a book from Amazon, say, or the week's groceries from Tesco.com.

Organizations can do this too, of course: the process is called '**e-procurement**' or '**B2B**' (business-to-business) and it is now very widely used for non-production purchases such as office supplies.

One-off organizational purchases may be made online in exactly the same way as an individual would make them, using an organizational credit card.

If online purchases are made regularly it is more likely that the organization will have an account with the supplier. An authorised and registered user will log in using a password and the organization will periodically be billed by the supplier. Depending on the status of the buying organization there may be discounts for volume purchasing or other special offers.

The supplying organization can set up its website so that it recognizes the purchaser once logged in and presents a list of 'favourites', i.e. items that the purchaser regularly buys. This saves searching for the items required and also avoids the need to key in name, address and delivery details.

B2B offers similar advantages to EDI in terms of speed and elimination of unnecessary work. It also offers the purchasing organization much wider choice than it might have had otherwise. In theory, resources can be sourced from suppliers anywhere in the world, perhaps at much lower prices than could be obtained if the organization only considered local suppliers.

For items where speed or cost of delivery is an issue it may not always be practical to order from a supplier in, for example, China, but a London firm, may find it gets better value if it orders from a supplier in Manchester rather than the local supplier it had used previously.

 Activity 28 · 3 mins

Can you see any potential problems for an organization that allows its purchasing department to use e-procurement?

_____

_____

_____

_____

The main issue is control: if anyone can order goods from anywhere there is a major risk that unauthorized purchases will be made. There is also an increased likelihood that purchases will be made from suppliers who cannot deliver the required quality (or cannot deliver at all!). For this reason, companies such as Ariba have developed special e-procurement software with built-in tools to control who can place orders at various spending levels, who orders should be placed with and so on.

2.5 Business exchanges

Following on from the success of e-procurement, organizations in many industries are now developing **business exchanges**. Typically an exchange gathers together the major enterprises in a given market sector — let's say, car manufacturing and creates a market-place of sufficient volume to attract increased numbers of suppliers.

All the participants in the formation of the exchange will ask their existing suppliers to join in, thus creating the beginnings of a supplier pool. If each participant adds their own existing suppliers then all participants will immediately be able to enjoy the benefits of increased choice and competition.

A notable example is Covisint, which brings together all the major motor manufacturers — Ford, General Motors, Nissan, Renault and so on.

3 Materials planning

For any sizeable organization, the problems of stock control and planning are considerable.

As we have seen, stock is a buffer between supply and demand; it may also be a considerable drain on the organization's finances.

One approach is to do without stocks altogether.

3.1 Less than the minimum: 'just-in-time'

A very large organization has considerable power over its suppliers, who can seldom afford to lose its custom. Knowing this, the organization with the huge buying power may, in effect, make the following statement to its suppliers:

EXTENSION 3
The radical approach to production is examined in David Hitchins' book.

'Sorry, we're no longer prepared to go to the trouble and expense of storing your products. From now on that's your problem.'

■ Supermarket retailers try not to hold stocks except on the sales floor; if they have a stockroom, it is purely a transit point where goods-in are received and checked before being put out on to the shelves.

Retailers will always say 'if the customers can't see it, it isn't selling', so it makes complete commercial sense to avoid holding stocks in a back room somewhere. The rule for retail stock ordering is 'little and often'.

■ Large manufacturing and assembly firms also try to do without having large stocks of components. They arrange for parts and materials to be delivered at exactly the time when they are needed, to be fed directly into the assembly lines.

These are called **just-in-time** (JIT) systems. The whole operation has to be highly organized to keep these large-scale enterprises fully stocked and running smoothly at all times.

Activity 29

3 mins

Write down **two** ways in which the JIT system differs from the traditional type of stores supply operation.

_____

_____

_____

_____

_____

_____

Perhaps the points you identified are among the following. Just-in-time systems depend on:

■ frequent and relatively small deliveries;
■ very short lead times;
■ close communication between the user and the supplier.

It may also have occurred to you that supermarkets that use just-in-time will also need:

- frequent, perhaps continuous, stock checks;
- computers to record the movement of goods in and out and to calculate the orders required;
- high-speed communication systems to transmit orders instantly to the suppliers.

Manufacturers that use just-in-time may depend on being able to:

- plan and forecast production rates;
- agree requirements in advance with their suppliers.

When the suppliers themselves need time to manufacture or assemble their products, advance planning is essential. The supplier and the user also need to communicate frequently in order to adjust and confirm the precise timing and volume of deliveries.

This is not possible without the aid of sophisticated technology, as the following real-life case history shows.

> A major car company, in its factory in the North East, has installed a system whereby a special coding tag on a car being built triggers a message to a supplier of carpets, boot linings and parcel shelves. There are 120 possible variations for these components, depending on colour, engine size, extras and whether the model is left-hand or right-hand drive. The component supplier has a factory just two miles away, and it makes deliveries up to 60 times a day.
>
> When the message is received by computer link, machines and operators at the supplier select, trim and fit plastic extras, before stacking them in sequence and loading them on trucks in small batches. On arrival, the driver takes the stock straight to the assembly line.
>
> The car manufacturer's management say that the system brings 100 per cent savings on inventory, 100 per cent savings on internal handling, and 90 per cent to 95 per cent savings on space, as well as productivity advantages. The dangers inherent in the system are also recognized. As the supplier's managing director says, 'If we failed to supply a part immediately it would shut down the plant.'

Activity 30

On the whole, just-in-time has been used only by large-scale businesses. Try to suggest **two** reasons why this is so.

_____

_____

Just-in-time is very inconvenient for suppliers, who are used to a world in which most of their customers (perhaps including your organization) are content to go along with the traditional way of doing things. This includes:

■ delivery during normal hours;
■ longish lead times;
■ grouped deliveries, perhaps covering several customers in an area;
■ largish order quantities, because of the long lead times;
■ buying and storing substantial stocks well in advance of when they are actually needed.

Large-scale just-in-time users have the power to insist on suppliers doing what suits **them**, such as:

■ delivery at any time of night or day;
■ frequent deliveries with very short lead times;
■ direct deliveries to them alone;
■ relatively small orders at a time.

In practice, vendors need to be located very close, geographically, to the organization they are supplying to.

However, it isn't only large manufacturing corporations that can benefit from the concepts behind JIT. In the past few years, some small and medium-sized hospitals have adopted a policy of having 'stockless inventory systems'. This involves moving some of the supply problems to the suppliers, and eliminating stock from the central storeroom. This brings benefits of reduced costs, but obviously needs careful management and reliable suppliers.

3.2 Materials requirements planning

In manufacturing companies, and in some service organizations, the concept of materials requirements planning (MRP) can provide a framework by which scheduling and inventory decisions are made.

MRP is:

- mainly concerned with the scheduling of activities, and the management of stock;
- most useful where components and sub-assemblies are produced, for incorporation in the final product or service.

Here are two examples of organizations that might benefit from applying MRP.

- A computer manufacturing company that assembles PC boards and buys in cabinets, which are brought together in the final product.
- A hotel, which provides not only accommodation but food, a bar service, dry cleaning and so on, in the packages it provides its guests.

In both these cases, the final product to the customer is **dependent** on the provision of lower-level goods or services.

If the number of customers is known or can be estimated, then the organization knows how many of each component must be manufactured, prepared or obtained. So one of the main inputs to the MRP process is a forecast demand. Its outputs are a detailed schedule of all the items that will be required, in order to make up the final product.

EXTENSION 4
If you would like to learn more about MRP, the book listed in this extension is a useful source of information.

The other inputs are the **bill of requirements** (or bill of materials), listing all the elements that go to make a product or service; **a schedule of capacity**, showing the capacity the organization has to make things; and a list of current stock.

The essential MRP structure is shown in the next figure.

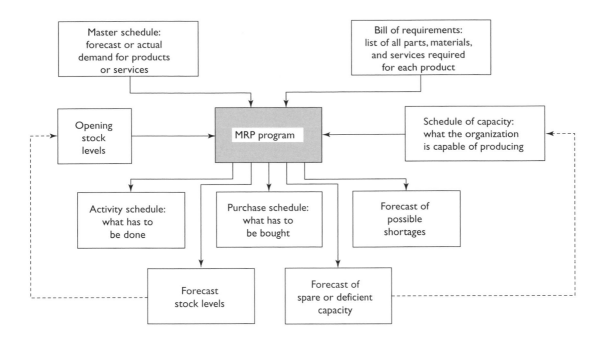

The centre box in this diagram is labelled the **MRP program** because the calculations are done by a software program on a computer. As with all computer programs, the accuracy of what you get out depends entirely on the accuracy of what you put in.

The program is run repeatedly, as new input data arrives.

Provided all the input data is correct, MRP is a very efficient method of scheduling and planning materials management. Prior to its use, materials and work scheduling was based on historical statistics, which was much less reliable.

4 Resource planning and management

Materials requirements planning was first introduced in the late 1980s at a time when only key areas of business were computerized – and 'computerized' meant specially written software running on mini or mainframe computers.

However, the introduction of low-cost networked PCs in the early 1990s opened up the possibility of linking up the activities of many more parts of the organization, and since that time we have seen steady advances in computerized methods of resource planning.

4.1 Manufacturing Resource Planning

As the name suggests, Manufacturing Resource Planning (sometimes called MRPII to distinguish it from MRP) does much more than simply plan materials requirements. Introduced in the early 1990s, it was a method for planning **all** manufacturing resources. Its starting point was the organization's business plans, and its outputs were detailed instructions for:

- the purchase department;
- suppliers;
- stores;
- the production staff.

In addition MRPII provided detailed financial plans, such as budgets and links to the financial accounting system.

MRPII software, together with networked PCs, linked together various, previously isolated functions, allowing manufacturing managers to obtain a complete picture of the activity and to set about optimizing the way the activity was performed.

In non-manufacturing industries similar approaches were adopted to help manage core areas.

4.2 Enterprise Resource Planning

As the effectiveness of various parts of a business was transformed, the spotlight shifted to the overall efficiency of the entire enterprise. As the technology of PC networking developed, the possibilities of supporting a larger version of MRPII, covering the entire enterprise, became more obvious.

Enterprise Resource Planning (ERP) offered the opportunity to share common data, and therefore the resources contained within the data, across a wide range of common activities, promising to repeat on an enterprise-wide basis the improvements gained in individual areas of activity.

Typical components of an ERP system are as follows.

■ Sales and distribution

This covers order entry and delivery scheduling. This module also checks on product availability to ensure timely delivery, and checks the customer's credit status.

■ Business planning

This consists of demand forecasting; planning of product production and capacity; and detailed routing information that describes where and in what sequence the product is actually made.

■ Production planning

Once the Master Production Schedule is complete, that data is fed into the MRP (Materials Requirements Planning) module: we looked at these earlier.

EXTENSION 5
Quayle and Jones' book looks at logistics from the point of view of those working in the distribution industry.

■ Shop floor control

The planned orders from the MRP module are converted to production orders. This leads to production scheduling, dispatching, and job costing.

■ Logistics

This system takes care of the rest, assuring timely delivery to the customer. Logistics in this case consists of inventory and warehouse management, and delivery. The purchasing function is also usually grouped under logistics.

Activity 31

4 mins

ERP systems have often failed to deliver the expected benefits when first implemented. Imagine that your organization is planning to adopt ERP. What possible problems might arise?

_____

_____

_____

_____

People are often the biggest barrier to the success of a new system. Staff may take the view that what they were doing before worked perfectly well and either not use the new system, or insist that it is adapted to reflect their old way of doing things, in which case few of the benefits of integration will be realized. Office politics may have a part to play in this.

Individuals also have much more responsibility when systems are closely integrated. The consequences of a mistake in one department are no longer restricted to that department: the implications could be much more widespread.

Another major problem is that existing systems in individual departments may not be compatible with each other. Short of throwing away all the data in one of the systems or re-entering vast amounts of data there may be no easy way of making different systems 'talk' to each other, or at least not at acceptable cost. (Some software vendors have developed Enterprise Application Integration, or EAI, to address such problems.)

You may have thought of other ideas specific to your own organization.

4.3 Supply Chain Management

Resource planning does not start and finish at the boundaries of the enterprise, so the next logical step has been to bring suppliers into the model at one end, and customers at the other end.

A 'supply chain' is a term used to describe how products or services move from an initial customer order through the various stages of obtaining any raw materials needed, putting them through production processes, and finally distributing the finished item to the customer. Numerous independent firms may be involved in a supply chain, for example manufacturers, components suppliers, delivery agents or shippers, wholesalers and retailers. Managing the chain of events in this process is called 'supply chain management'.

You may think that ERP software, as described above, covers the 'total material flow', but Supply Chain Management (SCM) software goes further. Although ERP systems provide a great deal of planning capabilities, the various material, capacity, and demand constraints are all considered separately, in relative isolation to each other.

SCM software helps to plan and optimize the supply chain as a continuous and seamless activity. SCM products are able to consider demand, capacity and material constraints simultaneously, and to perform real-time adjustments. Changes can be communicated instantaneously to all participants in the supply chain using Internet technology.

To give you a sense of the full capabilities of SCM software here is a list of the modules found in a typical SCM product from PeopleSoft.

Activity-Based Management	e-Procurement	Production Planning
Billing	e-Product Management	Promotions Management
Bills and Routings	e-Supplier Connection	Purchasing
Collaborative Supply Management	Flow Production	Quality
Cost Management	Inventory/Inventory Planning	SCM Portal Pack
Demand Planning	Order Management	Services Procurement
e-Bill Payment	Order Promising	Strategic Sourcing
Engineering	Product Configurator	Supply Chain Warehouse
Enterprise Planning	Production Management	Trading Partner Management

The idea of Supply Chain Management is not new – it was first mooted by Michael Porter in the 1980s – but the ability to micro-manage it in large organizations has only become a reality thanks to relatively recent developments in information and communications technology.

Moreover, in a modern business, supply chain management is more than just a piece of software. It is a change of attitude.

In the past the supply chain was typically defined by antagonistic relationships.

- The purchasing function sought out the lowest-price suppliers, often through a process of tendering, the use of 'power' and the constant switching of supply sources to prevent getting too close to any individual source.
- Supplier contracts featured heavy penalty clauses and were drawn up in a spirit of general mistrust of all external providers.
- The knowledge and skills of the supplier could not be exploited effectively: information was deliberately withheld in case the supplier used it to gain power during price negotiations.

Hence, no single supplier ever knew enough about the ultimate customer to suggest ways of improving the cost-effectiveness of the trading relationship, for instance buying additional manufacturing capacity or investing in quality improvement activities.

It is now recognized that successful supply chain management is based upon collaboration and offers benefits to an organization's suppliers as well as to the organization itself. By working together, organizations can make a much better job of satisfying the requirements of their end market, and thus both can increase their market share.

■ Organizations seek to enter into partnerships with key customers and suppliers so as to better understand how to provide value and customer service.

■ Organizations' product design processes include discussions that involve both customers and suppliers. By opening up design departments and supply problems to selected suppliers a synergy results, generating new ideas, solutions, and new innovative products.

■ To enhance the nature of collaboration the organization may reward suppliers with long-term sole sourcing agreements in return for a greater level of support to the business and a commitment to ongoing improvements of materials, deliveries and relationships.

Activity 32

4 mins

One of the main motivations for introducing Supply Chain Management will be financial. What do you think might be typical financial impact for an organization of SCM in terms of revenue and costs?

_____

_____

_____

_____

Here are some ideas that you may have included in your answer.

■ Reduced stock holding costs.
■ Reduced costs of purchasing.
■ Less waste because of better understanding of quality standards, and fewer errors.
■ Increased revenue due to higher quality product.
■ Increased revenue due to better/faster delivery performance.
■ Increased revenue due to new product ideas and products that more closely match customer needs.

Self-assessment 3

1 Fill in the missing words in the diagram below.

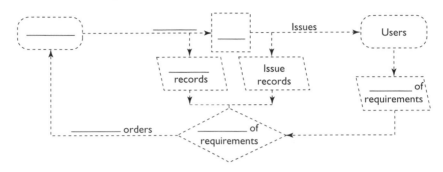

2 Match each name on the left with the correct comments, selected from the list on the right. More than one comment is associated with each name.

A Materials requirements planning (MRP)

B Electronic data interchange (EDI)

C Just-in-time (JIT)

D Automated guided vehicle (AGV)

a Enables buyers and suppliers to exchange a range of business documents including orders.
b Is concerned with the scheduling of activities and the management of stock.
c Is sometimes known as 'paperless trading'.
d May follow the path of wires laid beneath the floor.
e Produces schedules for activities and purchases as outputs.
f Produces forecast stock level as an output.
g Requires suppliers to make frequent deliveries, with very short lead times.
h Enables the customer to minimize stocks held in a waiting area.
i Causes the customer's stock-holding costs to be passed to the supplier.
j Is typically employed in moving heavy or palleted goods.

5 Summary

- The functions of purchasing include:
  - finding new suppliers;
  - minimizing the cost of purchases;
  - arranging for goods to be delivered when and where they are needed;
  - maintaining good relations with suppliers and with other parts of the organization.

- Electronic Data Interchange (EDI) is now used by many companies to speed up and control the exchange of business documents required when goods are bought and sold. Originally requiring specialist hardware and software, it was very expensive to run, but EDI is now available much more cheaply using the resources of the Internet.

- E-procurement, or B2B, is now also widely used for the purchase of non-production goods such as office supplies.

- Some businesses are using the potential of technology to create alliances for purchasing common requirements.

- The just-in-time system aims to minimize stock holding, and to demand supplies at the time and place they are needed, but not before they are needed. The system is only a practical proposition for large organizations with considerable 'buying power'.

- MRP (materials requirements planning) is:
  - mainly concerned with the scheduling of activities, and the management of stock;
  - is most useful where components and sub-assemblies are produced, for inclusion in the final product or service.

- Inputs to an MRP program are: the master schedule; a bill of requirements; the opening stock balances; a schedule of capacity. Outputs are: an activity schedule; a purchase schedule; a shortage list; forecast stock levels; forecast of spare or deficient capacity.

- MRPII (manufacturing resources planning mark II) goes much further than MRP, in that it is a method for planning all manufacturing resources.

- Enterprise Resource Planning (ERP) looks at the potential for increasing efficiency by sharing common data across the whole enterprise.

- Supply Chain Management uses software to bring suppliers into the chain of management of materials and resources, thus optimizing the supply chain.

- Security management should flow from a clear statement of policy, backed with appropriate resources and proper organization and arrangements, including training at all levels and the clear indication that disciplinary action will be taken against any employee who breaches the policy.

- Risk assessments and frequent use of the 'what if' question are essential elements of professional security management. The potential consequences of identified risks must be dealt with on the basis of tackling the 'worst first'.

- Professional risk management will deter most potential offenders and save time in any investigations.

- The most important single aspect of security is the attitude of managers, who must set the right example to employees, contractors and customers at all times.

- Restricting access to stock and sensitive areas and disseminating information on the 'need to know' principle are important aspects of a security policy.

- Careless talk in an organizational security context can cost livelihoods.

- Complete security is an unachievable goal for any organization – the cost would outweigh the value of the savings achieved.

Session D
Managing waste

1 Introduction

Within every type of organization the processes of work will result in waste.

Valuable resources can be wasted in a number of ways, including:

- misuse – used for a purpose for which they were not designed, resulting in inefficiency and shortages for their intended purpose
- extravagance – where a resource is being consumed even though it is not necessary in order to achieve objectives
- scrap – items left over as a result of a production process which cannot be readily used elsewhere
- rework – where items have to be remade because they failed quality controls
- shrinkage – where the resource is consumed in unauthorized ways (often used as a euphemism for 'theft'), where it deteriorates in quality over time, or simply becomes obsolescent.

Elimination of waste will not be practical across all work processes, but reduction of waste in many of these is desirable.

Types of waste will fall within the four categories of resource examined throughout this workbook. These categories are:

- people
- capital
- materials
- information.

We usually associate the idea of waste with the materials resource category. Although we will focus on this particular aspect of waste for the purpose of this session it is important not to lose sight of the fact that waste can, and does, occur in each of the remaining three categories.

EXTENSION 6
A useful website giving information about waste management is given at the end of this workbook.

People are not used efficiently across the work processes, whether we consider manufacturing or service industries. Individual capabilities are not always recognized and used to best effect, or development is not offered to enable individuals to maximize their contribution to the business as a whole; and so there is waste. Business assets or capital may be misused because they are not always suitable or appropriate to the current or future needs of that business. The business may not invest sufficiently in its equipment or machinery, requiring staff to spend time repairing or 'making-do', resulting in customer dissatisfaction and ultimately loss of money, another example of waste.

Information produces waste as well, in situations where businesses do not gather, exchange or indeed use information in a way which is relevant to how the business functions. Many businesses suffer from information overload, where there is a great deal of information available, but not enough that exists in the detail and format that everyone can use efficiently. This is a clear, and common, example of waste.

This session will focus primarily on the area of materials waste, exploring methods for measuring and monitoring it, as well as setting out practical approaches to the minimizing of it.

2 Waste control legislation

A range of regulations and legislation are in place in relation to waste disposal which will have varying levels of impact on your own area of work.

The European Union has passed legislation to underpin and improve waste handling controls, including:

- Packaging Waste Regulations
- Landfill Levy
- Fridges and Ozone Depleting Regulations
- Environmental Protection Act (1990).

Activity 33

Which of these legislative and regulatory areas apply to your organization as a whole, and to your area of work in particular?

_____

_____

_____

Briefly describe what the requirements are. (You may need to talk to your manager or human resources department to get this information.)

_____

_____

_____

_____

How do you currently ensure that your area of work conforms to the regulations as required?

_____

_____

How satisfied are you that you and your staff understand the implications of these regulations and laws?

_____

_____

Although the nature of your business may not necessitate you understanding the requirements of each of these items, within each there may be aspects which apply, and which will affect your plans for waste reduction and waste disposal.

3 The costs of waste

There are a range of costs associated with waste, its production and its minimization.

Waste has costs that are usually stated in terms of monetary loss to the organization. Most organizations rarely calculate the true monetary cost of waste. The Environment Agency considers that the actual cost of waste can be as high as 5–10 per cent of company turnover (Source: The Environment Agency; *www.environment-agency.gov.uk* June 2002). Businesses regularly underestimate the cost of waste to their business and in doing so have no clear picture as to real loss of profit.

Activity 34 · 4 mins

Other than the monetary cost of waste what other costs can you identify? Try to make three suggestions.

_____

_____

_____

You could have mentioned:

- rework of poorly finished items
- lost stock – raw material, contributory items
- quality and reduced customer satisfaction
- waste handling and disposal
- environmental – within the company and on a wider basis
- need for protective clothing, monitoring and handling equipment, where hazardous substances form part of the work process
- insurance to cover liabilities in relation to waste disposal and emissions
- monitoring of waste.

You may have identified others which are relevant to your area of work, and which do not appear in the above list.

The Environment Agency offers a definition of the true cost of materials waste as:

'the cost of the raw material in the waste added to the cost of disposal'.

In a wider sense we could include labour, processes, energy, consumables, etc. within the 'raw materials' description to get a clearer indication of what needs to be considered.

In a production scenario we would need to calculate this cost in relation to every item produced, which can seem both time consuming and potentially difficult. If businesses fail to carry out this calculation they lose sight of where savings can be made and where money can be reclaimed within the work processes. In terms of a service situation the calculation is as valid, if not as apparently straightforward.

Activity 35

3 mins

> All contributory factors within a work process need to be taken into account when calculating the cost of waste.

Within a service sector business, what might be included in the term 'raw materials' when examining the definition of materials waste?

_____

_____

_____

The list is extensive, but could include factors such as:

- time, possibly including travel time where, for example, salespeople need to visit client premises
- people, where staff regularly find themselves with insufficient work to do
- information, including too much irrelevant information
- access to equipment, such as computers and telephones
- consumables, such as stationery
- fuel for vehicles, again relating to the example of salespeople travelling.

4 A staged approach to managing waste

The most important part of implementing any programme of waste reduction is to gain the commitment of both senior management **and** all staff.

Commitment from senior management will support any need for using time, and possibly the need for capital investment, where this proves essential. Staff commitment will reduce any potential barriers that may lie in the way of programme success.

Waste reduction is an ongoing process and is less likely to succeed where it is perceived as a one-off initiative. Contributions from everyone will form the basis of this success. As we have already identified the costs of waste and the factors affecting waste permeate all aspects of work, and so everyone can make active contributions to waste reduction.

The stages in managing waste are as follows:

1   Awareness raising

2   Process analysis

3   Clarifying costs

4   Future planning

5   Defining the problem and identifying solutions

6   Taking action.

These stages do not stand alone. For example, awareness raising cannot be a stage in its own right, as it is essential that everyone is made constantly aware of the issues, while being informed as to the actions they will need to take.

We will explore each of these stages in some detail so that you can consider how you might proceed with each one in your own area of work.

5 Awareness raising

An awareness campaign that sets out the benefits of waste reduction, while emphasizing the range of costs associated with waste, is a useful way of focusing attention on waste minimization. Individuals can be encouraged to identify sources of waste in their own area, and to offer suggestions for how waste might be reduced. It is important to encourage enthusiasm for the whole idea of waste reduction, but it can be all too easy for this to become a one-off campaign which quickly loses momentum and which is not deemed an important everyday issue.

A waste reduction awareness campaign can usefully kick-start awareness raising. Ongoing reminders of the importance of waste reduction will be essential to keeping the process alive within the business.

Activity 36 · 3 mins

List three advantages of reducing waste that you believe would arouse staff interest in supporting a waste reduction programme.

_____

_____

_____

The advantages will vary greatly from business to business, team to team. Some of the ideas you had might have included:

■ reduced frustration when less time has to be spent having to rework badly finished products
■ reduction in customer complaints because the quality of service and products improves

■ heightened respect from the community where they see the business investing in improving the local environment through improved approaches to waste disposal.

Each of these points arises from the success of different waste reduction programmes in different types of organization. Using these ideas you may now wish to go back to the activity you have just finished and add further ideas for arousing staff interest.

6 Process analysis

In order to analyse each of the work processes in your area you will need to consider the following questions.

■ What kinds of waste are produced from this area of work?
■ How much of each type of waste is produced on a weekly/monthly/quarterly/ annual basis?
■ What methods of waste disposal are used?
■ What environmental requirements do we need to take into account when disposing of business waste?

Activity 37 · 10+ mins

Design a form that covers each of the above questions and has sufficient space for responses. (For the second question you might want to limit the timescales, for example you may just ask for information regarding waste production on a monthly basis.) Then issue the form to key individuals within each area of work which falls within your supervision, and ask them to complete it and return it to you.

One obvious means of raising awareness is to involve staff in gathering responses to these questions. Again, the nature of the business will affect certain responses to a greater degree than it will do in others. However, this type of investigation will not only heighten awareness, but will help to inform where the business has fallen into bad habits, or indeed where the business has failed to take account of the ever-increasing environmental legislation which affects it.

The responses to the questions will help in identifying the range of actual work processes which produce waste. Process analysis is a method of mapping out each of the actions that go into any work process.

We will use the following illustration as an example of how a process can be analysed.

A chiropodist will need an appointment system in order to improve people by attending to their feet. The stages in this chiropodist-client booking process may include:

Stage 1   advertise chiropody service in local paper/mailshot to existing clients.

Stage 2   receive phone calls from clients.

Stage 3   input appointments into diary (book or computer).

Stage 4   greet clients and place them in waiting room.

Stage 5   take clients through to chiropodist.

A flowchart is an effective and efficient means of carrying out and illustrating process analysis.

One way of illustrating each stage of this process is by producing a flowchart. Each box of the flowchart will contain a separate stage, with arrows going between each in the relevant direction.

To develop a fuller analysis of each process you can include detail on which raw materials are needed at each stage. For example, in stage 2 above (receive phone calls from clients) such materials would include a telephone, receptionist and, probably a computer.

Example:

```
2 Receive phone calls from clients
            receptionist
             telephone
        notepad/computer/diary
```

In order for the process analysis to be thorough the flowchart will need to show:

- each stage in the process
- the raw materials and resources needed for each step.

As well as this information the flowchart will also need to show points where waste is or could be produced.

These points can appear as crosses or exclamation marks next to the box containing the relevant stage.

Example: Chiropodist client booking process

```
3 Greet clients and place in waiting room
              receptionist
                 chairs
        magazines/radio/sound system!
```

From the information gathered earlier, possibly by using questionnaires as designed in Activity 37, you will have a clear indication of where waste occurs and the nature of this waste.

Activity 38 · 3 mins

Why do you believe an exclamation mark might appear next to stage 3 in the chiropodist–client booking process?

_____

_____

You may have said that, assuming that there is only one chiropodist available, there is never likely to be more than one client waiting at any one time. The size of the waiting room may be over and above that required, and the space may be better used by increasing the reception area itself, or even by giving the space to the chiropodist through reorganization of the existing space. At the same time if there is only one client the sound system may be superfluous, when up-to-date magazines would allow the client to fill in the short waiting time quite adequately.

The number of stages in each process will vary, and so of course will the complexity of the resulting flowchart. It is important to try and keep the process analysis simple and easy to understand – your flowcharts will provide valuable visual information to others, and serve to illustrate points of actual or potential waste.

Activity 39 · 10 mins

Refer back to the completed forms that asked individuals to identify types and sources of waste (Activity 37). From this information identify up to three separate work processes. Choose one of these and draw a flowchart that clearly illustrates:

■ each stage in the process
■ raw materials and resources required at each stage
■ points where waste is or could be produced.

7 Clarifying costs

This stage in the waste minimization process refers you back to the information in section 3, *The costs of waste*, and to the work that you have already done in Activity 37. You were asked to consider the real costs of waste within your area of work. Now reconsider these in the light of the detail offered in section 6, *Process analysis*.

Activity 40

20+ mins

Refer back to the flowchart which you produced for Activity 39.

1 List the types of cost associated with this process. If possible provide detail of the actual costs (for example, costs of receptionist) on an hourly basis.

2 Now consider the location of waste production and estimate the potential cost of this waste where it is identified. For example, provision of a superfluous sound system.

3 Where waste disposal is associated with waste, estimate the costs of waste disposal across the complete process.

You may or may not have detailed information to support the completion of this activity, but even if you are only able to estimate the costs you will be building a clearer picture of the real costs of waste.

Activity 41

Reconsider your flowchart. What potential or actual cost savings might be the result of any waste reduction, where it has been identified as feasible?

Type of potential waste reduction	Potential/actual costs savings

As others become more actively involved in identifying and tackling issues of waste, waste-related costs will reduce accordingly.

8 Future planning

If you have already identified a number of areas for immediate waste reduction, or are in the process of taking the necessary action to reduce waste effectively and efficiently, it is likely that you are already seeing signs of increased efficiency across the work processes that you have analysed. In order to develop efficiency overall there will be some areas where immediate action is not practical. Any list that you have started to build will need to be prioritised, so that a resulting action plan, as at stage 6 of the waste management process, will take account of the necessary resources.

When establishing priorities for your list, consider the following questions.

- What are the immediate costs of reducing waste?
- What capital costs might be needed?
- What disposal costs are attached to waste reduction?

- What environmental impact will result from the waste reduction, for example are there any proposed process changes or materials usage that will fall within legal or regulatory controls?
- What impact will these changes have on other work processes, and will this hinder efficiency elsewhere?

(Based on The Environment Agency 9 Step Process for Waste Minimization, June 2002.)

By involving other members of your team in considering these questions, you will not only develop support for these proposed changes, you will also access their knowledge of the particular issues.

It is important to remember that this list of potential waste reduction areas is in fact a list of potential changes. The earlier you can involve others in determining feasibility the more likely any changes are to succeed.

9 Defining the problem and identifying solutions

This is another stage that does not fit neatly into a strict process. This stage involves identifying **why** waste is the result of particular stages in the work process, and then identifying how best to reduce this waste. As you will realize this will already have begun to happen throughout the other stages, particularly during process analysis.

Activity 42

Identify two areas where waste is being generated (you might want to refer to the flowchart which you drew in response to Activity 39), and briefly respond to the following questions for each area.

- What is happening to create this waste?
- When is the waste being generated; at exactly which stage of the work process?

■ What would happen further down the work process if this level of waste were eliminated?

Area 1 _____

_____

_____

Area 2 _____

_____

_____

9.1 Cause and effect

We are now coming to the point of considering the causes of the waste and its effect.

Activity 43

25 mins

Discuss your responses to the previous activity with others within your team. Now ask them the following questions.

It is important to prioritize any list of potential changes; involving others in this process will ensure that resulting changes are dealt with positively.

■ What is the actual cause of the waste that is being generated?
■ What is the real effect of the waste?

Write a full description of the actual cause and the real effect of the waste that is being generated. Your aim is to write a description that gives a thorough picture of the situation. This description becomes your definition of the waste reduction issue. Try and write the definition in language which makes sense to everyone concerned, in this way you will help people relate to what is required, helping them to feel that they can make a sound contribution to any proposed solutions.

A good and clear definition of the waste reduction issue will provide a useful starting point for arriving at practical solutions.

Once the waste reduction issue has been clearly defined it is essential to identify reasonable and practical solutions to this issue. As stated earlier it will be beneficial to involve others, drawing on their knowledge and expertise of the issue, its causes and its effects.

Activity 44 · 1 hour

Call a meeting of those who are affected by the waste reduction issue, or perhaps involved in the cause. Ask: what can we do to address this waste reduction issue? Produce a list of **all** the suggestions offered.

Consult everyone, exploring the suggestions on the list.

Through this consultation:

1 Eliminate those suggestions which are obviously impractical or ill-advised.

2 Rank the remaining suggestions in three groups where group 1 = most practical, group 2 = practical and group 3 = feasible.

The resulting list will be a ranked list of suggestions which already have the support both of those concerned and of those who are essential to the success of any changes made.

 10 Taking action

By this stage you will have comprehensive information on the points where waste is being generated, a definition of the causes and effects of this waste generation, and a list of potential solutions or means of waste reduction. You will have realized that stages 4, 5 and 6 are closely inter-linked.

You are now in a position to create an action plan to reduce the identified waste. We have given an example of an action plan below.

Waste reduction issue	Action required	Responsible person	Timescale	Review date	Evaluation	Desired outcome
1. Reduce quantity of A4 copier paper rejected at office copier and thrown into wastepaper bins	a. Set up copy logging system	Andi	w/c 12 June	17 June	Log completed and register numbers tally	Reduce copier paper orders by 5% within next two quarters
	b. Collect re-usable paper from copier and staple into notepads	Ben	Twice daily from w/c 12 June	Twice weekly from w/c 12 June	Only paper which cannot be salvaged to be found in wastepaper bins	
	c. Train all office staff in use of photocopiers to reduce errors	Ellie	Completed by 26 June	26 June	All staff able to operate photocopier and reduce errors of use	

As a means of ensuring that action is taken regularly and on an ongoing basis, a simple action plan will establish:

- the waste reduction issue
- steps required to reduce the waste
- who has responsibility for taking the necessary steps
- timescales against which the steps will be taken
- milestone points, review dates
- methods of evaluation
- desired outcome.

Activity 45

5 mins

What can you do to ensure that your waste reduction action plans are implemented? Try to make three suggestions.

_____

_____

_____

> Waste reduction can only result from practical and well-considered action.

You will have recognized that the key factors in ensuring action plan implementation will include:

■ sound definition of the waste reduction issue, which everyone concerned can understand and relate to
■ a series of realistic stages that will result in waste reduction
■ allocation of responsibility for different stages given to those who are able to take the necessary action
■ ensuring that those with allocated responsibility have the relevant authority and access to the necessary resources
■ review dates adhered to
■ evaluation methods suited to the types of action required
■ the desired outcome set in terms that are measurable.

Self-assessment 4 ·

10 mins

Fill in the blanks in the following sentences with suitable words chosen from the list below.

(a) Most organizations rarely calculate the true _____ cost of waste.

(b) All _____ factors within a work process need to be taken into account when calculating the cost of waste.

(c) A waste reduction _____ can usefully kick-start awareness raising. Ongoing reminders of the _____ of waste reduction will be essential to keeping the process alive within the business.

(d) A _____ definition of the waste reduction issue will provide a useful starting point for arriving at practical _____ .

RELEVANT	GOOD AND CLEAR	FINANCIAL
CONTRIBUTORY	SMART	MONETARY
ENJOYMENT	AWARENESS CAMPAIGN	SOLUTIONS
	IMPORTANCE	RESULTS

2 List the six stages in managing waste reduction.

_____

_____

_____

_____

_____

_____

3 Identify three key factors in ensuring that waste reduction action plans are implemented.

_____

_____

_____

Answers to these questions can be found on page 110.

11 Summary

- The costs which result from the generation of waste include:

  - monetary cost of waste
  - rework of poorly finished items
  - lost stock – raw material, contributory items
  - quality and reduced customer satisfaction
  - waste handling and disposal
  - environmental – within the company and on a wider basis
  - need for protective clothing, monitoring and handling equipment
  - insurance to cover liabilities in relation to waste disposal and emissions
  - monitoring of waste.

- Waste reduction is an ongoing process, rather than just a one-off initiative.

- By adopting a staged approach to waste reduction, success is more likely.

- A staged model for waste reduction includes the following six stages:

  1 awareness raising
  2 process analysis
  3 clarifying costs
  4 future planning
  5 defining the problem and identifying solutions
  6 taking action.

- An awareness campaign that sets out the benefits of waste reduction while emphasizing the range of costs associated with waste is a useful way of focusing attention on waste minimization.

- Process analysis includes questioning what is happening and identifying where waste is created.

- A flowchart setting out each work process should include:

  - each stage in the process
  - raw materials and resources required at each stage
  - points where waste is/could be produced.

- Costs need to be clarified in order to produce a real picture of the actual costs of the waste itself, and the disposal of this waste.

- Future planning will enable ideas for waste reduction to be carefully prioritized.

- By defining the problem you will begin to consider cause and effect, i.e.

  - what is the actual cause of the waste that is being generated?
  - what is the real effect of the waste?

- An action plan for reducing waste will need to include:

  - the waste reduction issue
  - steps required to reduce the waste
  - who has responsibility for taking the necessary steps
  - timescales against which the steps will be taken
  - milestone points, review dates
  - methods of evaluation
  - desired outcome.

Performance checks

1 Quick quiz

Jot down the answers to the following questions on Managing the Efficient Use of Materials

Question 1   We listed nine types of resource. Name **five** of these.

_____

_____

_____

_____

_____

Question 2   Why might it be dangerous to treat people as just another resource?

_____

_____

_____

Question 3   What would you say to someone who wanted some good general advice on getting the best from equipment?

_____

_____

_____

Question 4   Explain the differences between raw materials, components and consumables.

_____

_____

_____

Question 5   Explain briefly what is meant by the statement: 'having stocks too high is bad news; having stocks too low may be worse news'.

_____

_____

_____

Question 6   What is meant by 'shrinkage'?

_____

_____

_____

Question 7   Write down the book stock formula.

_____

Question 8   What is the purpose of ABC analysis?

_____

_____

_____

Question 9   Which **two** main types of transaction take place as a result of goods being received?

_____

_____

Question 10   What is the meaning of 'minimum stock'?

_____

_____

_____

Question 11   'There are no real advantages for an organization in having a person or group that specializes in purchasing.' Briefly explain the reasons why you do, or do not, agree with this statement.

_____

_____

_____

Question 12   Name **one** advantage, and **one** disadvantage, of the just-in-time system, from the point of view of the organization being supplied.

_____

_____

_____

Question 13   List **one** input, and **two** outputs, of an MRP program.

_____

_____

_____

_____

Question 14   What are the six stages of waste reduction?

_____

_____

_____

_____

_____

_____

Question 15   What are the three key features that a process flowchart needs to illustrate?

_____

_____

_____

Answers to these questions can be found on pages 111–12.

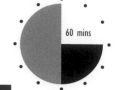

2 Workbook assessment

Read the following case incident and then deal with the questions that follow, writing your answers on a separate sheet of paper.

AC Electrics is an independent company that, in its one plant, produces about 150 different consumer products. In many cases, the difference between the products is only slight and the result of some modification. For example, they produce twelve models of vacuum cleaner.

The consumer market is extremely competitive and so it is essential, if it is to survive, for the firm to adopt a market-oriented policy. This is even more important for AC Electrics as they are one of the smaller firms in this business. To this end AC Electrics sell directly to wholesalers and large retailers throughout the country. These customers expect a high level of service and often require very fast deliveries. In order to meet these demands, AC Electrics established a number of regional warehouses, where stocks of all the products are held.

Three departments have responsibility for the control of stock.

■ The marketing department is responsible for the control of all finished goods both in the warehouses and at the plant. Through their direct contacts with existing and prospective customers and their market-research activities, they claim to be able to forecast the stock levels required for each product in each warehouse.
■ The production department is responsible for the control of stock required for production and also for work-in-progress. Production requirements consist mainly of bought-in components, together with a few raw materials such as packaging. The department's principal concern is to meet promptly the requirements of the marketing department to supply the regional warehouses. In order to meet this aim, production plans often have to be changed at relatively short notice.
■ The other department which has responsibility for stocks within AC Electrics is the purchasing department; this is concerned with maintenance stocks and works and office supplies. It does the buying for the production department. The purchasing department is not entirely happy with the short-term planning of the production department and its effect on purchasing costs. Generally, they believe that the organization is paying too much for components and materials, and that costs could be reduced if they could place orders in larger quantities.

1 Identify the likely costs associated with the above method of holding stocks.

2 Suggest **two** ways in which some of these costs might be reduced.

3 What advantages would AC Electrics gain by adopting a system of materials management such as MRP?

4 Do you think that stock-holding costs could be wholly or partly passed along to AC Electrics' suppliers? Explain your answer.

Reflect and review

1 Reflect and review

Now that you have completed your work on *Managing the Efficient Use of Materials*, let us review our workbook objectives.

This was our first objective.

■ When you have completed this workbook you will be better able to contribute to the management and control of resources in your organization.

We have looked, if only briefly in some cases, at a number of resources, and have highlighted a number of associated problems. As a manager, one of your principal functions is to organize and control resources effectively and efficiently.

Although we didn't devote much space to the management of people in this workbook, a couple of very important points were noted: the difficulties of developing people to their full potential; and the dangers of regarding employees as inanimate objects, to be handled without respect for their dignity as human beings.

Equipment, land, buildings, and materials, all require careful management, and, in the case of the first three, we identified a few ways in which they might be usefully dealt with.

Our main concern, however, has been with materials, and we have considered many aspects of the management of this resource.

You might like to think about the answers to the following questions.

■ How could you increase your skills in the management of people?

_____

_____

_____

_____

■ How could you set about finding out more about the management of some of the other resources mentioned: equipment, time, energy, finance, land, buildings, information?

_____

_____

_____

_____

■ What will be your first step in contributing further to the control of resources in your organization?

_____

_____

_____

_____

The second objective was as follows.

■ When you have completed this workbook you will be better able to explain the principles, and some ways of solving the problems, of stores and stock control.

The purpose of a store is as a buffer between the supplier and the user: between supply and demand. Holding stock, as we discussed, does not come cheap. In any small or medium-sized organization, however, it is an almost inescapable function. For large corporations, the costs and problems may be pushed onto the suppliers, using JIT.

Technology may help, and the increasing use of computers and other electronic devices, certainly enables organizations to reduce shrinkage and over-stocking. Useful techniques include those of ABC analysis, better documentation, and stock rotation. Everyday efficiency by teams and team leaders can do wonders for cost control.

■ Which of the stock control techniques described in the workbook might be appropriate for your organization? How might you investigate it further?

_____

_____

_____

■ Write down **one** problem in stores or stock control that you know about. How could you set about solving it?

_____

_____

_____

The third objective was as follows.

■ When you have completed this workbook you will be better able to increase your skills in various aspects of materials management.

Materials management entails much more than stores and stock control, and effective organizations take a broad-based view of the subject. Purchasing is one area: how can materials be obtained at minimum cost? In the production of goods and services, how can plans be made so that all operations run more efficiently? Would increased automation be an answer?

You may not be in a position to make large-scale plans for your organization, but you can try to improve the way things are run in your own work area, and you can take steps to increase your own knowledge and skills.

■ What specific aspects of materials management should you study further? How will you go about doing this?

_____

_____

_____

The fourth objective was as follows.

■ When you have completed this workbook you will be better able to identify risks to physical, human and information resources and have gained some practical ideas and experience with which to guard against them.

All managers have a responsibility for the security of the resources which they manage, including the 'human' resources. You have had opportunity to look at a number of aspects of this vast subject, which perplexes not only commercial organizations but governments throughout the world, including the following.

■ The varied nature of security risks and their repercussions.
■ The five-step risk management approach to security management and the use of 'what if' questions to help you plan for contingencies.
■ The need to balance security considerations against the safety rights of people who need to escape rapidly from buildings.
■ The need to apply 'common sense' strategies to prevent opportunist or audacious attempts to breach security.
■ The restriction of access to premises, stocks and information to protect security.
■ The mistake in believing that insurance means that losses 'don't matter' or that losses don't matter because 'it's only company property'.
■ The increasing need to guard against malicious attacks on personnel.
■ The costs v. savings balance and the threat of business closure when costs of security become unsustainable.
■ The need for a security policy published to and applicable to personnel at all levels, backed up by the example which managers set to their staff at all times.

What specific messages will you take from this session and apply to make your own work area secure, or recommend for use more widely within your organization?

_____

_____

_____

The final objective was:

■ You will be better able to carry out a review of actual and potential waste generation points and take action to reduce waste accordingly.

Waste will be generated at different points of every work process and this waste will relate to each of the four resource areas – people, finance, capital and materials.

You might like to ask yourself the following questions.

■ Where can I see immediate areas for waste reduction within my area of work?

_____

_____

_____

■ What can I do to get my team involved in and committed to active waste reduction?

_____

_____

_____

2 Action plan

Use this plan to further develop for yourself a course of action you want to take. Make a note in the left-hand column of the issues or problems you want to tackle, and then decide what you intend to do, and make a note in column 2.

The resources you need might include time, materials, information or money. You may need to negotiate for some of them, but they could be something easily acquired, like half an hour of somebody's time, or a chapter of a book. Put whatever you need in column 3. No plan means anything without a timescale, so put a realistic target completion date in column 4.

Finally, describe the outcome you want to achieve as a result of this plan, whether it is for your own benefit or advancement, or a more efficient way of doing things.

Desired outcomes				
1 Issues	2 Action	3 Resources	4 Target completion	
Actual outcomes				

3 Extensions

Extension 1

Book *Storage and Supply of Materials*
Author David Jessop and Alex Morrison
Edition 7th edition 2003
Publisher FT Prentice Hall

Jointly published with the Chartered Institute of Purchasing and Supply, this book 'seems to be firmly established as the standard book for practitioners and students ... The contents have generally been brought up to date, with greater emphasis on health and safety and to relevant EC directives ...' It is not difficult to read, and would be very useful to have on hand as a reference book, and something to dip into when you have time.

Extension 2

Standard *BS EN ISO 9001:2000 Quality management systems. Requirements*
Publisher British Standards Institution

There was formerly a British Standard directly concerned with stock control (BS 5729) but this has been withdrawn, no doubt because it was published in the 1980s and bore little relation to current practice.

However, the latest version of the well-known international quality management standard, BS EN ISO 9001, contains a number of very relevant sections. Here is a brief note of the parts of BS EN ISO 9001 that are particularly relevant to controlling physical resources.

- **6.3 Infrastructure**
This section contains requirements about maintaining buildings, workspaces, and equipment.
- **7.4.1 Purchasing process**
This encourages organizations to set up controls to ensure that purchased products meet materials specifications and that their suppliers meet supplier selection criteria.
- **7.4.2 Purchasing information**
These requirements encourage proper record-keeping. Purchasing documents should clearly describe the product ordered.
- **7.4.3 Verification of purchased product**
This section sets out requirements to verify incoming materials at your own organization's premises and/or at the suppliers' premises. (Verify means to perform whatever checks and tests are necessary to make sure that the purchased items meet your organization's specifications.)
- **7.5.3 Identification and traceability**
Purchases should be identifiable from the time they are received throughout all the stages of production, delivery and installation.

■ **7.5.4 Customer property**

This section reminds organizations to identify, verify and safeguard property supplied by their customers, for instance if the customer sends in a product for repair.

■ **7.5.5 Preservation of product**

This section requires you to take steps to avoid damage to products and components during production and on final delivery, for instance by using proper packaging, by refrigerating perishable items, or by handling fragile items with care.

Extension 3

Book	*Just in Time*
Author	David Hutchins
Edition	2nd edition, 1999
Publisher	Gower Publishing Limited

Just In Time is not just another way of organizing stock control, but a radical change in the production methods and in the role of employees. They have to take far more responsibility for production, which in turn requires their commitment and enthusiasm. This book looks at all these aspects and shows how the purchasing and stock control functions have to change to support JIT.

Extension 4

Book	*Essentials of Operations Management*
Author	Ray Wild
Edition	Fifth edition, 2001
Publisher	The Continuum International Publishing Group

This book covers all aspects of the operations and production management function, with a number of useful case studies to show how it inter-relates to the purchasing, supply, logistics and materials handling functions, in the use of systems such as JIT, MRP and automated handling.

Extension 5

Book	*Logistics: an Integrated Approach*
Author	Michael Quayle & Bryan Jones
Edition	1998
Publisher	Liverpool Academic Press

Focusing on the supply chain from the physical distribution perspective, this book will be particularly useful to those people working in the distribution industry who want to develop their understanding of how their role relates to other supply chain functions.

Extension 6

More information on waste management can be found on http://www.defra.gov.uk/environment/waste/index.htm

These extensions can be taken up via your ILM Centre. They will either have them or will arrange that you have access to them. However, it may be more convenient to check out the materials with your personnel or training people at work – they may well give you access. There are other good reasons for approaching your own people; for example, they will become aware of your interest and you can involve them in your development.

4 Answers to self-assessment questions

Self-assessment 1 on pages 18–20

1 Compare your ticks with the table below.

	Materials	Equipment	People	Buildings	Land	Information	Energy	Finance	Time
Land					✓		✓		
Capital	✓	✓		✓		✓		✓	
Labour			✓						✓

2 The complete list is as follows.

The management of resources involves:

1 **DECIDING** what you want to achieve;
2 making **PLANS** to achieve it;
3 **SPECIFYING** the necessary resources;
4 locating and **ACQUIRING** those resources;
5 **PREPARING** the resources;
6 **CONTROLLING** and organizing the resources to best effect.

3 The completed puzzle is as follows:

Self-assessment 2 on pages 50–1

1 The only reason for holding stock is to have it ready for when it is needed. Because most goods take time to acquire (the lead time), they may have to be ordered well in advance in order to bridge the gap between the supply and the demand.

2 The completed boxes are as shown.

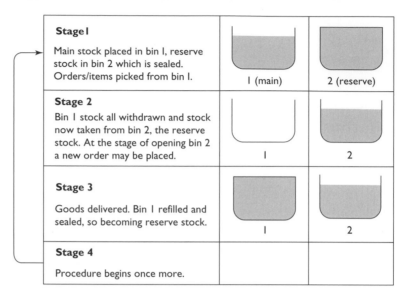

Stage1 Main stock placed in bin 1, reserve stock in bin 2 which is sealed. Orders/items picked from bin 1.	1 (main)	2 (reserve)
Stage 2 Bin 1 stock all withdrawn and stock now taken from bin 2, the reserve stock. At the stage of opening bin 2 a new order may be placed.	1	2
Stage 3 Goods delivered. Bin 1 refilled and sealed, so becoming reserve stock.	1	2
Stage 4 Procedure begins once more.		

3 The usage values are as follows.

Item	Unit cost (£)	Annual sales	Usage value (£)
Vacuum cleaner	230	500	115,000
Microwave oven	340	750	255,000
Refrigerator	175	330	57,750
Installing kit	25	1000	25,000
Spares kit	45	120	5,400

4 ABC analysis is a means of categorizing items of stock on the basis of their usage value, where usage value is the cost of the item times the number issued or sold annually. ABC analysis is a modification of the Pareto principle, which shows that the bulk of value is likely to be held by a very small proportion of the total items. When the Pareto principle is applied to stock management, we usually adopt three categories, A, B and C, rather than the two categories of 80:20.

5 The completed sentences are as follows.

a Stock is a **BUFFER** between supply and **DEMAND**, or between the suppliers and the users.

    b Organizations generally aim to keep the **MINIMUM** stocks in the minimum **SPACE** for the minimum time.

    c Having stocks too **HIGH** is bad news; having stocks too **LOW** may be worse news.

    d Opening stock + **PURCHASES** − issues = closing stock.

    e In any store, about **20 PER CENT** of all the items held will account for about **80 PER CENT** of the usage value.

6 a When receiving goods, a goods received note (GRN) is needed. Purchasing need the GRN to check the supplier has delivered the goods ordered. Accounts need the GRN to arrange payment.

    b The minimum stock is the lowest possible level you should hold to avoid running out. The safety stock is lower than the minimum stock. The organization re-orders so that safety stock is not eaten into. However, since it *is* safety stock if, for example, a delivery is unexpectedly late, some safety stock may be used.

Self-assessment 3 on page 71

1 The completed diagram is as follows.

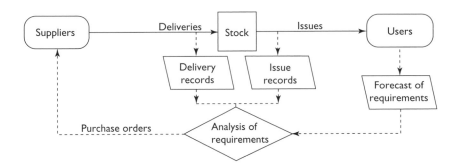

2 A Materials requirements planning (MRP)

        b Is concerned with the scheduling of activities and the management of stock.

        e Produces schedules for activities and purchases as outputs.

        f Produces forecast stock level as an output.

    B Electronic data interchange (EDI)

        a Enables buyers and suppliers to exchange a range of business documents including orders.

        c Is sometimes known as 'paperless trading'.

    C Just-in-time (JIT)

        g Requires suppliers to make frequent deliveries, with very short lead times.

        h Enables the customer to minimize stocks held in a waiting area.

        i Causes the customer's stock-holding costs to be passed to the supplier.

D Automated guided vehicle (AGV)

    d May follow the path of wires laid beneath the floor.

    j Is typically employed in moving heavy or palleted goods.

Self-assessment 4 pages 190–1

1 a Most organizations rarely calculate the true MONETARY cost of waste.

  b All CONTRIBUTORY factors within a work process need to be taken into account when calculating the cost of waste.

  c A waste reduction AWARENESS CAMPAIGN can usefully kick-start awareness raising. Ongoing reminders of the IMPORTANCE of waste reduction will be essential to keeping the process alive within the business.

  d A GOOD AND CLEAR definition of the waste reduction issue will provide a useful starting point for arriving at practical SOLUTIONS.

2 The six stages in managing waste reduction are:

1 Awareness raising
2 Process analysis
3 Clarifying costs
4 Future planning
5 Defining the problem and identifying solutions
6 Taking action.

3 Key factors in ensuring that waste reduction action plans are implemented include:

- sound definition of the waste reduction issue, which everyone concerned can understand and relate to
- a series of realistic steps that will result in waste reduction
- allocation of responsibility for different steps needs to be given to those who are able to take the necessary action
- ensuring that those with allocated responsibility have the relevant authority and access to the necessary resources
- review dates are adhered to
- evaluation methods suit the types of action required
- the desired outcome is set in terms which are measurable.

5 Answers to activities

Activity 13 on page 30

Perhaps you didn't have much trouble in answering as follows.

a 140 (opening stock) + 120 (purchases) − 160 (issues) = 100 (closing stock).
b Opening stock + purchases − sales = closing stock.
c 90 + 60 − 70 = 80.
d Opening stock + purchases − closing stock = issues (sales).

6 Answers to the quick quiz

Answer 1   You could have mentioned: people; equipment; land; buildings; finance; materials; information; energy; time.

Answer 2   The simple answer is that people do not respond well when they feel they are being treated like a piece of furniture or equipment. Managers who fall into this trap seldom succeed in their aims.

Answer 3   To get the optimum value from equipment, it is important for the people using it to have: a good understanding of what it is designed to do; training in how to use it; a proper system of maintenance; an appropriate system of security.

Answer 4   Raw materials are basic substances that are processed in order to manufacture products, such as wood and plastics. Components are parts, often having themselves been manufactured from raw materials, which go to make a larger assembly. Consumables are items that are used up in a work process, and do not necessarily form part of the final product.

Answer 5   If stocks are too high, money is tied up in goods that aren't being used. If stocks are too low, the organization's activities may be impeded, which may be potentially even more costly.

Answer 6   Shrinkage is losses and deterioration caused by: a decline in quality; goods becoming out of date; damage; pilferage.

Answer 7   The book stock formula is expressed as follows:
            opening stock + purchases − issues = closing stock

Answer 8   ABC analysis is a method of determining the relative amount of attention that should be given to goods in stock. (You might also have mentioned that a usage value is calculated for each item, which is the purchase price times the number issued or sold; the highest usage value items receive the greatest amount of attention.)

Answer 9   There are two possible transactions involved in the receipt of goods: taking in new goods, just delivered by a supplier; and taking back old goods, which had been issued and which are now being returned for some reason.

Answer 10   The minimum stock is the lowest possible level you should hold to avoid any danger of running out.

Answer 11   There are real advantages to having purchasing specialists, including the facts that: it is a job requiring a good deal of expertise; it is important to build up good relationships with regular suppliers, and this takes time and effort; a specialist will be able to find suppliers for new items quickly; non-specialist managers won't waste time on purchasing tasks, which they have no training in.

Answer 12   Potential advantages include: lower inventory costs, lower handling costs, lower space costs, and increased productivity. Disadvantages are that it may be difficult to implement unless your organization has a lot of 'buying power', a great deal of planning is required, and if things ever go wrong, business may effectively come to a halt.

Answer 13   Inputs are: the master schedule (a forecast or actual demand for products or services); a bill of requirements (a list of all parts, materials, and services required for each product); the opening stock balances; a schedule of capacity (what the organization is capable of producing). Outputs are: an activity schedule (what has to be done); a purchase schedule (what has to be bought); a shortage list; forecast stock levels; forecast of spare or deficient capacity.

Answer 14   The six stages of waste reduction are:

1 Awareness raising.
2 Process analysis.
3 Clarifying costs.
4 Future planning.
5 Defining the problem and identifying solutions.
6 Taking action.

Answer 15   The three key features that a process flowchart needs to illustrate are:

1 Each stage in the process.
2 Raw materials and resources required at each stage.
3 Points where waste is/could be produced.

7 Certificate

Completion of this certificate by an authorized person shows that you have worked through all the parts of this workbook and satisfactorily completed the assessments. The certificate provides a record of what you have done that may be used for exemptions or as evidence of prior learning against other nationally certificated qualifications.

superseries

Managing the Efficient Use of Materials

....

has satisfactorily completed this workbook

Name of signatory ....

Position ....

Signature ....

Date ....

Official stamp

Pergamon
Flexible
Learning

Fifth Edition

superseries

FIFTH EDITION

Workbooks in the series:

Achieving Objectives Through Time Management	978-0-08-046415-2
Building the Team	978-0-08-046412-1
Coaching and Training your Work Team	978-0-08-046418-3
Communicating One-to-One at Work	978-0-08-046438-1
Developing Yourself and Others	978-0-08-046414-5
Effective Meetings for Managers	978-0-08-046439-8
Giving Briefings and Making Presentations in the Workplace	978-0-08-046436-7
Influencing Others at Work	978-0-08-046435-0
Introduction to Leadership	978-0-08-046411-4
Managing Conflict in the Workplace	978-0-08-046416-9
Managing Creativity and Innovation in the Workplace	978-0-08-046441-1
Managing Customer Service	978-0-08-046419-0
Managing Health and Safety at Work	978-0-08-046426-8
Managing Performance	978-0-08-046429-9
Managing Projects	978-0-08-046425-1
Managing Stress in the Workplace	978-0-08-046417-6
Managing the Effective Use of Equipment	978-0-08-046432-9
Managing the Efficient Use of Materials	978-0-08-046431-2
Managing the Employment Relationship	978-0-08-046443-5
Marketing for Managers	978-0-08-046974-4
Motivating to Perform in the Workplace	978-0-08-046413-8
Obtaining Information for Effective Management	978-0-08-046434-3
Organizing and Delegating	978-0-08-046422-0
Planning Change in the Workplace	978-0-08-046444-2
Planning to Work Efficiently	978-0-08-046421-3
Providing Quality to Customers	978-0-08-046420-6
Recruiting, Selecting and Inducting New Staff in the Workplace	978-0-08-046442-8
Solving Problems and Making Decisions	978-0-08-046423-7
Understanding Change in the Workplace	978-0-08-046424-4
Understanding Culture and Ethics in Organizations	978-0-08-046428-2
Understanding Organizations in their Context	978-0-08-046427-5
Understanding the Communication Process in the Workplace	978-0-08-046433-6
Understanding Workplace Information Systems	978-0-08-046440-4
Working with Costs and Budgets	978-0-08-046430-5
Writing for Business	978-0-08-046437-4

For prices and availability please telephone our order helpline   +44 (0) 1865 474010
or email   directorders@elsevier.com